CGP is the <u>only</u> choice for KS3 English!

KS3 can feel like a whirlwind of information, but with this brilliant Workbook from CGP, perfecting your English skills will be a breeze.

There are warm-up questions at the start of each section to recap what you know, followed by buckets of practice to hone your reading and writing abilities. Everything's split into topics, so you can concentrate on the areas you find tricky.

After that you can have a crack at the review sections to show off what you've learnt. You'll also find all the answers at the back. Handy. Almost like we planned it.

CGP — still the best! ☺

Our sole aim here at CGP is to produce the highest quality books — carefully written, immaculately presented and dangerously close to being funny.

Then we work our socks off to get them out to you
— at the cheapest possible prices.

Contents

How To Use This Book..1

Section 1: Reading — Audience and Purpose
Before you Start..3
Audience...4
Purpose...5
Context...6

Section 2: Reading — Non-Fiction Texts
Before you Start..7
Finding Evidence in the Text...8
Making Inferences..9
Layout and Structure..10
Language Techniques...11
Tone..13
What You Think..14
The Author's Intentions..15

Section 3: Reading — Fiction and Plays
Before you Start..16
Finding Evidence in the Text...17
Making Inferences..18
Structure...19
Themes...20
Language Techniques...21
Characterisation...22
Setting..24
Interpreting Plays...26
Staging and Performance...28
What You Think..29

Section 4: Reading — Poetry
Before you Start..30
Making Inferences..31
Structure...32
Themes...33
Voice...34
Techniques...35
Interpreting Poems...36
Comparing Poems..38

Section 5: Reading — Comparing Texts
Before you Start..39
Comparing Texts..40

Contents

Section 6: Reading Review
Frankenstein by Mary Shelley 44
Blessing by Imtiaz Dharker 46
Macbeth by William Shakespeare 48
The Simulation — *Dreams of Somewhere* 50

Section 7: Writing — Non-Fiction Writing
Before you Start 52
Planning 53
Structure 54
Quoting 56
Writing Essays 57
Formal and Informal Language 59
Writing to Inform, Explain and Advise 60
Writing to Persuade and Argue 62

Section 8: Writing — Fiction Writing
Before you Start 64
Planning 65
Structure 66
Building Character 67
Building Setting 68
Writing Stories 69
Writing Scripts 70
Poetry 71

Section 9: Writing — Writing Properly
Before you Start 72
Structuring Your Writing 73
Redrafting and Proofreading 74

Section 10: Writing — Making It Interesting
Before you Start 75
Using Different Techniques 76
Figurative Language 77

Section 11: Writing Review
Writing Review 78

Answers 82

Published by CGP

Editors:
Emma Cleasby, Rachel Craig-McFeely, Rebecca Greaves, Katya Parkes,
Hannah Roscoe, Rebecca Russell, Kirsty Sweetman

Acknowledgements:

Extract on page 18: Copyright © Matt Haig, 2013 Extracts from THE HUMANS
reproduced with permission of Canongate Books Ltd through PLSclear.

Extract on page 22: "Pan's Labyrinth: The Labyrinth of the Faun" by Guillermo del Toro and Cornelia Funke,
2020, Bloomsbury Publishing Plc.

Extract on page 23: "A Raisin in the Sun" by Lorraine Hansberry, 2011, Bloomsbury Publishing Plc.

Extracts on page 25: The Book Thief by Markus Zusak © 2016.
By arrangement with the licensor, Markus Zusak, c/- Curtis Brown (Aust) Pty Ltd.

Extract on page 26: THE CRUCIBLE by Arthur Miller. Copyright © Arthur Miller, 1952, 1953, 1954.
Copyright renewed © Arthur Miller, 1980, 1981, 1982. Earlier version copyright under the title
THOSE FAMILIAR SPIRITS, used by permission of The Wylie Agency (UK) Limited.

Page 30: Poem "What If This Road" by Sheenagh Pugh © originally published in 'Ids Hospit' published by Seren Books (1997).
Used with permission of the author and Seren Books.

Page 32: Poem "Praise Song for My Mother" by Grace Nichols from
'I have Crossed an Ocean: Selected Poems' (Bloodaxe Books, 2010)

Page 33: Poem "The City of my Birth" by Karl Nova from 'Rhythm and Poetry'
– with kind permission from Karl Nova and Caboodle Books

Page 34: Poem "To Travel This Ship" by James Berry from 'A Story I Am In: Selected Poems' (Bloodaxe Books, 2011)
Reproduced with permission of Bloodaxe Books. www.bloodaxebooks.com

Page 35: Poem "Cats" by A. S. J. Tessimond from 'Collected Poems' (Bloodaxe Books, 2010)

Extract on page 41: "Rebecca" by Daphne du Maurier. Reproduced with permission of Curtis Brown Ltd, London,
on behalf of The Chichester Partnership. Copyright © 1938 The Chichester Partnership

Page 46: Poem "Blessing" by Imtiaz Dharker from 'Postcards from God' (Bloodaxe Books, 1997)
Reproduced with permission of Bloodaxe Books. www.bloodaxebooks.com

A note for teachers, parents and caregivers

Just something to bear in mind if you're choosing further reading for Year 9 pupils
— all the extracts in this book are suitable for children of this age, but we can't
vouch for the full texts they're taken from, or other works by the same authors.

ISBN: 978 1 78908 785 7

With thanks to Claire Boulter and John Sanders for the proofreading.
With thanks to Jan Greenway for the copyright research.

Clipart from Corel®
Printed by Elanders Ltd, Newcastle upon Tyne

Based on the classic CGP style created by Richard Parsons.

Text, design, layout and original illustrations © Coordination Group Publications Ltd. (CGP) 2021
All rights reserved.

Photocopying this book is not permitted, even if you have a CLA licence.
Extra copies are available from CGP with next day delivery • 0800 1712 712 • www.cgpbooks.co.uk

How To Use This Book

- Hold the book <u>upright</u>, approximately <u>50 cm</u> from your face, ensuring that the text looks like <u>this</u>, not this. Alternatively, place the book on a <u>flat</u> surface (e.g. a table or desk) and sit in front of the book, at a comfortable distance that doesn't make the text too small to read.
- In case of emergency, press the two halves of the book together <u>firmly</u> in order to close.
- Before attempting to use this book, familiarise yourself with the following <u>safety information</u>:

Different schools cover different Key Stage 3 English topics at <u>different times</u>. <u>Don't panic</u> if you come across something you haven't learnt yet — just <u>skip</u> that topic and move on.

The book is split into two parts — <u>Reading</u> and <u>Writing</u>. In the Reading section, you'll be answering questions based on <u>texts</u>. In the Writing section, the questions will help you improve your <u>writing skills</u> and write some of <u>your own stuff</u>.

There are <u>eleven sections</u> covering different topics, so it's easy to find questions on the <u>specific thing</u> you want to practise.

Every question has an <u>answer</u> at the back of the book — the answers start on page 82.

Each section starts with some <u>quick questions</u> to refresh your memory of <u>key skills</u> and show you what to expect in that section.

There are some <u>hints</u> to help you answer <u>specific questions</u>.

How To Use This Book

Each topic has a page or two of questions that get more challenging as you work through them.

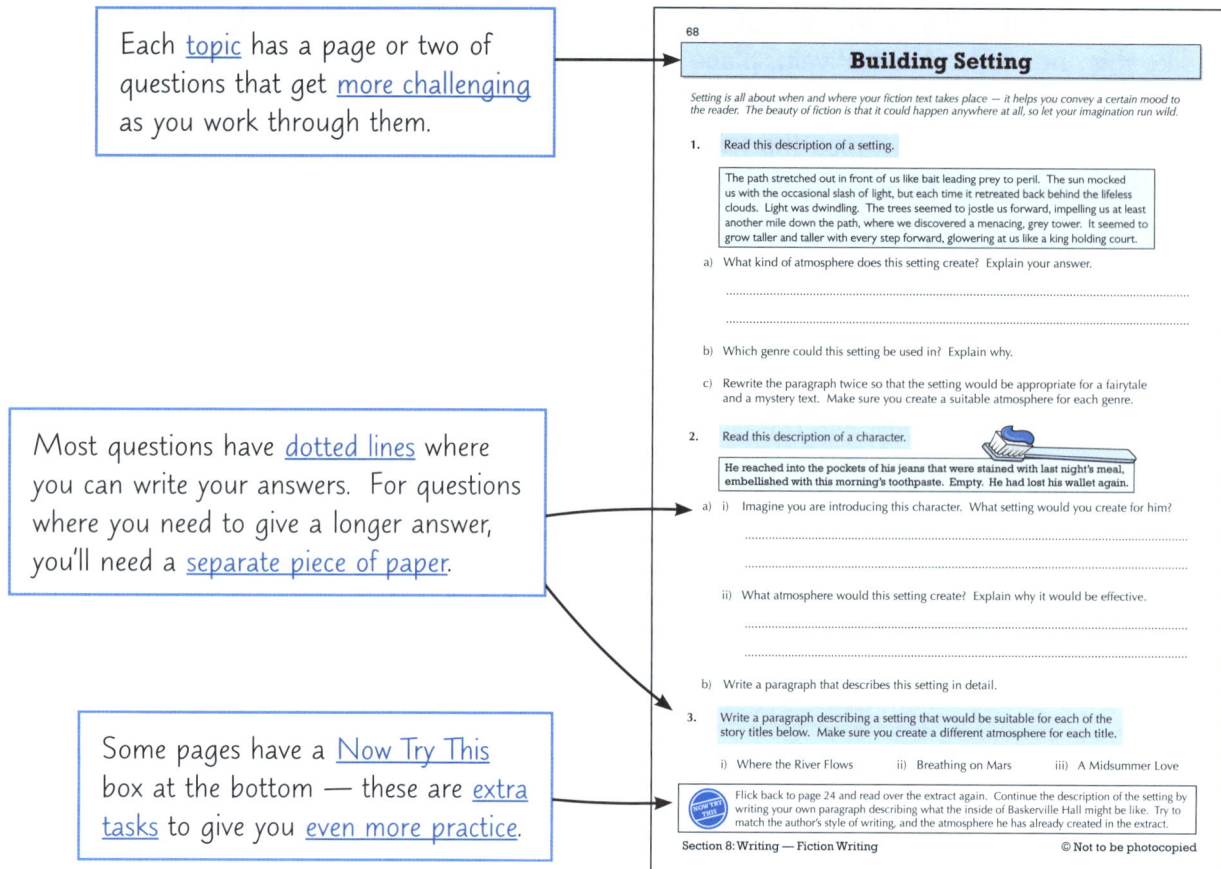

Most questions have dotted lines where you can write your answers. For questions where you need to give a longer answer, you'll need a separate piece of paper.

Some pages have a Now Try This box at the bottom — these are extra tasks to give you even more practice.

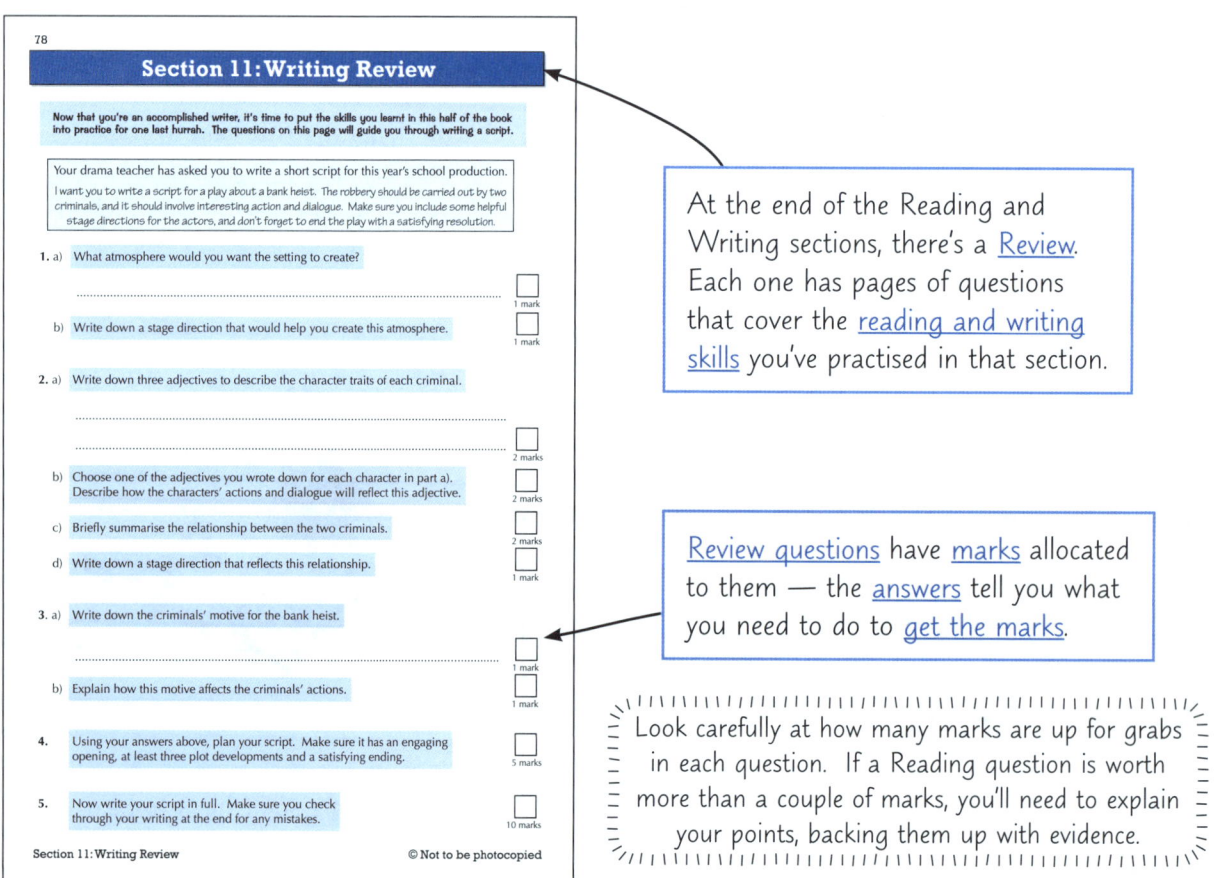

At the end of the Reading and Writing sections, there's a Review. Each one has pages of questions that cover the reading and writing skills you've practised in that section.

Review questions have marks allocated to them — the answers tell you what you need to do to get the marks.

Look carefully at how many marks are up for grabs in each question. If a Reading question is worth more than a couple of marks, you'll need to explain your points, backing them up with evidence.

How To Use This Book

Section 1: Reading — Audience and Purpose

Every time you read a text, consider its audience and its purpose. These two things have a big impact on the content of a text and its features — oh, how I dream that one day I can make as much impact...

Before you Start

1. Read the following text about airports.

   > Trust me, going through an airport isn't as complicated as it seems. Just make sure you're organised — have your passport ready and put any small bottles of liquid in a clear plastic bag ready for inspection. Then, once you're on the plane, sit back, relax and enjoy your flight!

   a) Write down the intended audience of this text.

   ....

   b) Explain your answer to part a).

   ....

   ....

2. The following extract is from a newspaper article.

   > Authorities have issued a warning to residents of Skipham regarding Joe's Diner. The premises have been cordoned off due to a sudden explosion of raw sewage through the drain in the kitchen, which then flowed into the diner. After petrified customers had fled the scene, Joe remarked that the diner was merely in need of "minor sanitisation".

   a) What is the purpose of this text?

   ....

   b) How does the purpose of this text affect its style? Explain your answer.

3. Read this passage about the novel *Of Mice and Men* by John Steinbeck.

   > The novel *Of Mice and Men* was influenced by the 'American Dream': a lifestyle focused on ambition and material success that many Americans desired. While Steinbeck shows that poor migrant workers dream of owning their own farms, the harsh reality of life during the Great Depression of the 1930s suggests that the 'American Dream' is only an illusion.

   a) Underline an example of cultural context in the passage.

   b) Write down an example of historical context from the passage.

   ....

Audience

Writers choose the style, content and layout of a text in order to suit a particular audience. If they don't bear the audience in mind, they might not fully get their point across. It's nice to be thought of, isn't it?

1. The extract below is about an alternative form of navigation.

   > One of the leading experts in our field, Leo Shone, announced today that he is preparing to sail from the UK to Canada using only celestial navigation. Leo hopes to be the fastest man to travel this route using traditional navigation methods, and is said to be fond of using Cassiopeia, rather than The Big Dipper, to locate Polaris. This could work in his favour, as you might understand if you recall the complications of Celeste Sink's ill-fated 1972 voyage.

   a) Who is the intended audience of the text?

   b) Explain how you can tell that the text has been written for this audience.

   ....

   ....

2. The letter below has been written to a mayor by a citizen of their town.

   > Dear Mayor Smith,
   >
   > I am writing to you about a matter of extreme urgency. I firmly believe that your proposal to demolish the old Barefield mansion constitutes nothing less than a grave error.
   >
   > Firstly, it is the only historical site remaining in this town, whose history has consistently been stripped away in so-called 'improvements' by local authorities. Surely you agree that ridding the town of its history will leave future residents with no sense of the past?
   >
   > Secondly, and most importantly in my opinion, the mansion is believed to be home to vengeful spirits. Admittedly, this rumour is borderline ludicrous, but I would warn you not to disregard it completely. Quite frankly, the last thing we need is paranormal activity spreading around town.
   >
   > Yours sincerely,
   > Polly Chapman

   a) Briefly describe the language style in this letter.

   ....

   b) How has the author structured the letter to emphasise their concerns?

   c) Explain why the features you identified in a) and b) are appropriate for this letter.

   d) How would you rewrite the letter if you were addressing a close friend?

 Write a speech to deliver at a local primary school informing pupils about the importance of reporting bullying. Make sure you use features that are appropriate for your audience — think about the style of language you use, the information you include and the tone of your speech.

Section 1: Reading — Audience and Purpose

Purpose

Texts are written for a whole host of reasons — to entertain, persuade, advise, inform, you name it. I'm writing to inform you about English, but frankly, I think I was born to entertain. One of these days...

1. The text below is an extract from an advert for a hotel.

   > Alleviate the stress of your daily life by visiting Brighton's most luxurious seaside hotel! Our award-winning facilities are guaranteed to thoroughly revitalise your mind and body through a regime of total rest and relaxation — or your money back! With a chance like this at your fingertips, how can you resist? Contact our remarkable resort now for affordable prices that will leave both you and your bank account pleasantly surprised.

   a) Write down an example of each of the following persuasive techniques from the extract.

   rhetorical question: ....

   direct address: ....

   b) Choose one of the techniques from part a) and explain why it is effective.

   ....

   ....

2. The extract below is from a speech.

   > Extensive use of social media is having a more detrimental effect on our wellbeing than we think. Reports claim that over 3 billion of us are social scrollers, many of us hooked on the high of likes, shares and stories. Ultimately, social media is far too new for us to truly fathom its consequences for future life, so we must act now to limit the grasp it has on us. Without imposing daily limits now, we *will* become prisoners to our phones.

   a) A text can have more than one purpose. What are the two main purposes of this text?

   ....

   b) Write down two techniques the writer has used to achieve these purposes.

   ....

   ....

   c) Why are each of these techniques effective?

 Imagine you're going to write a letter to Year 6 pupils advising them about life in secondary school. Make a list of features you could use in the letter to make it effective. Think about tone, language and structure. Now have a go at writing the letter, using the features you've listed.

© Not to be photocopied   Section 1: Reading — Audience and Purpose

Context

It's handy to know what was going on at the time a text was written or is set (its historical context) and the way of life at this time (its cultural context) — this can help you to better understand the ideas in the text.

1. The text below is an abridged extract from Charlotte Perkins Gilman's short story, *The Yellow Wallpaper*. It was written in 1890 and is narrated by an unnamed woman.

   > If a physician of high standing, and one's own husband, assures friends and relatives that there is really nothing the matter with one but temporary nervous depression — a slight hysterical tendency — what is one to do?
   >
   > So I take phosphates or phosphites — whichever it is, and tonics, and journeys, and air, and exercise, and am absolutely forbidden to "work" until I am well again.
   >
   > Personally, I disagree with their ideas.
   >
   > Personally, I believe that congenial work, with excitement and change, would do me good.
   >
   > But what is one to do?
   >
   > I did write for a while in spite of them; but it *does* exhaust me a good deal — having to be so sly about it, or else meet with heavy opposition.

   a) What impression do you get of the relationship between men and women in the 1800s?

   ....

   ....

   b) How does the author show this relationship?
   Explain your answer using details from the extract.

2. This is an extract from the poem *The Cry of the Children* by Elizabeth Barrett Browning.

   > Go out, children, from the mine and from the city —
   >   Sing out, children, as the little thrushes do —
   > Pluck you handfuls of the meadow-cowslips pretty
   >   Laugh aloud, to feel your fingers let them through!
   > But they answer, "Are your cowslips of the meadows
   >   Like our weeds anear the mine?
   > Leave us quiet in the dark of the coal-shadows,
   >   From your pleasures fair and fine!"

   In the 19th century, it was common for children in Britain to be employed in mines and factories. This poem was written in 1843, shortly after a law was passed that restricted the use of child labour in mines.

   a) What does this extract suggest about the lives of child workers in the 19th century?

   ....

   ....

   b) Explain your answer to part a), using evidence from the extract.

   c) Why do you think Elizabeth Barrett Browning wrote this poem? Explain your answer.

Section 2: Reading — Non-Fiction Texts

Time to delve into the familiar world of non-fiction. These are the texts you encounter every day — reading a film review, following your favourite brownie recipe, you name it. Non-fiction texts really are everywhere. Have a go at the warm-up questions below and prepare to become non-fiction-fixated.

Before you Start

1. The extract below is from a text about black holes.

    > Black holes are one of the most exciting fields of research in astronomy. A black hole forms when a giant star comes to the end of its life, culminating in the very centre of the star collapsing and triggering an explosion called a supernova. After this explosion, the newly formed black hole consumes gas, dust, and even other stars, growing more and more substantial over time.
    >
    >
    >
    > Gravity is so strong inside black holes that nothing (not even light) can escape from their inky depths, meaning they're invisible to the human eye — they can only be 'seen' because of how objects around them behave.
    >
    > There are different types of black hole: miniature, stellar, intermediate and the biggest of them all, supermassive. These are estimated to be millions of times bigger than the Sun.
    >
    > It is thought that there is a supermassive black hole at the centre of almost every galaxy in the universe. The one in the Earth's galaxy (the Milky Way) is referred to by astronomers as 'Sagittarius A*', and it is estimated to be 4.6 million times bigger than the Sun.

    a) i) What is the text's purpose?

        to advise ☐   to inform ☐   to persuade ☐   to entertain ☐

        ii) Explain why you have ticked this box.

        ....

    b) i) Write down three words to describe the text's tone.

        ....

        ii) Explain why you have chosen these words.

        ....

    c) Why can't humans see black holes?

        ....

    d) In your own words, summarise the first paragraph of the text.

Finding Evidence in the Text

In an essay, points are the lead singer — the band needs them. But quotes are the backing dancers and, in all honesty, the lead singer would look rubbish without them. So always give your points some support.

1. The extract below is from a travel article about La Sagrada Família in Barcelona.

> ### A bit about the building...
> The unparalleled Sagrada Família, or as I call it, 'the unfinished church', has been under construction since 1882, and what do you know — it's still going! The church was designed by an architect named Antoni Gaudí, who oversaw the project from 1883 until he passed away in 1926. Progress has been slow because the construction relies on donations to fund it.
>
> It's predicted the building will be finished in the next decade, after well over a century of construction. Don't let the ongoing work stop you from visiting before then though, as observing its painstaking progress in action only adds to the building's unique and iconic charm.
>
> ### Getting there...
> If you like a walk, the church is about half an hour from the city centre, or there are various buses that will take you there. This is less efficient than going by the good old Metro though.
>
> ### When you're there...
> A ticket to go inside will set you back a fair few pennies, but from experience, going inside is worth it not only for the decadent interior, but also for a much-needed break from the Spanish sun. One thing's for sure — you won't be let down by the staggering sights of the Sagrada's awe-inspiring architecture (even half-finished), so make sure you don't leave it off your schedule. It's not one you want to miss!

a) When did construction under Gaudí begin?

....

b) 'The author thinks the ticket prices are high.' Find a phrase that supports this statement.

....

c) Find evidence from the text which suggests that Barcelona has a warm climate.

....

d) Explain why the author uses each of the adjectives below to describe La Sagrada Família. Use details from the text to support your answers.

| iconic | decadent | staggering |

e) i) Write down at least three words or phrases that show that the text is written in an informal tone.

....

ii) Why do you think the author has used an informal tone?

Section 2: Reading — Non-Fiction Texts

Making Inferences

Some texts are a little bit shy on the details, so you have to infer bits of information yourself to gain a full understanding of what's going on. Use your powers of deduction to find the invisible information.

1. The extract below is from an autobiography.

   > On the tracks I was flourishing, but at school I was always running just a little bit behind everyone else. I sat on my own and daydreamed the hours away — I didn't appreciate that studying books and solving equations were important skills too. My parents didn't mind too much. They were swallowed up by two lots of nappies and two lots of formula milk — they had other battles to fight.
   >
   > I liked the track because it was a place just for me. I was free to revel in my glorious independence, and there was nobody there to tease me for being by myself. With every training session, my personal bests were improving and my ambition was bubbling over. My body was only growing stronger, and each time I thought I'd reached my limit, I only went faster. I was enthralled by the power I could feel just by moving my body.
   >
   > Everyone has always thought I was motivated by winning, by prize money, by medals, but actually I was just driven by the way it made me feel. I've found little else over the course of the years that has been as loyal to me as my sport.

   a) What career did the author have? How can you tell?

   ....

   ....

   b) Do you think the author did well at school? Support your answer with details from the text.

   ....

   ....

   c) What can you infer from the following phrase about the author's parents?

   "They were swallowed up by two lots of nappies and two lots of formula milk"

   ....

   d) What do you think the author's relationship with their peers was like?
   Explain your answer using details from the text.

   e) What does the last paragraph tell you about people's perceptions of the author?

   f) Do you think the author has been successful in their career? Explain your answer.

 Now you've made several inferences from the extract above, it's time to have a go at putting them to use. Write a short newspaper article about the person in the extract, using information that you've inferred about their life from the text. You can invent your own details about them too.

© Not to be photocopied   Section 2: Reading — Non-Fiction Texts

Layout and Structure

A key feature of non-fiction writing is how text is arranged on a page, and the order of that information. Writers specifically design layout and structure with a text's purpose in mind. Oh, they are good to us...

1. The extract below is a job advert.

   > ### GRAPHIC DESIGNERS WANTED
   >
   > APPLY NOW
   >
   > - **Bored** of working for a faceless, corporate company?
   >   Graphik-wire is a **vibrant**, close-knit agency **bursting** with **passion** for our field.
   > - **Overflowing** with creativity?
   >   Graphik-wire sees creativity and **innovation** as a **cornerstone** of what we do.
   > - **Desperate** to be part of an innovative team?
   >   Graphik-wire is all about **cooperation**, **partnership** and team **synergy**.
   >
   > The good news is, we are **HIRING!**
   >
   > We are looking for passionate design visionaries to join our growing team of enthusiastic creatives. As the city's biggest design agency, we strive to deliver the highest quality service for our brands, with a unique approach to the industry.
   >
   > Send a portfolio and CV over to us today!

   a) i) Which sentence best describes how the information in the text is structured?

   It is written in chronological order. ☐

   It poses a problem to the reader and offers a solution. ☐

   It is disordered to indicate that the job is chaotic. ☐

   Don't forget — layout is about how the information looks. Structure is about how the information is ordered.

   ii) Use evidence from the text to explain why you ticked this box.

   b) Do you think the use of bold text is effective? Explain your answer.

   ....

   ....

   c) Find two more layout devices used in the text. Explain why the author has used them.

   d) How does the writer directly address the reader? Explain your answer.

   ....

   ....

   e) Do you think the layout and structure effectively support the text's purpose? Is there anything that you would change?

Language Techniques

The language techniques writers include are usually strategic choices — they use them to affect the reader in specific ways. You need to identify what techniques are used, and the purpose they serve in the text.

1. The extract below is from a newspaper report.

   > **CHIMP'S PAINTING HITS THE JACKPOT**
   >
   > A chimpanzee broke records this week when its painting, 'Artistic Decisions', sold for £500 000 at auction. Chai the chimp learnt to paint over a year ago and has since created more than 15 pieces of art at his home in the sunny state of Florida.
   >
   > This isn't the first time a chimpanzee's painting has found success, but never has one sold for such a sizeable sum. Chai's triumph has led many on social media to label him as "the greatest animal artist of our generation".
   >
   > Chai's keeper, Fiona Gibbon, says she was overcome when she heard about the bid. "It was astonishing — I couldn't believe it. He genuinely enjoys spending time in front of his easel. Some of the chimps I look after like to be a bit mischievous but Chai is an angel. All he ever wants to do is work on his canvasses."
   >
   > Chai has received several commissions since the exhibition. Many have likened his creative style to the Expressionists.
   >
   > When asked about Chai's future in art, Fiona had this to say: "Well, the paintings speak for themselves. I think we want to get an exhibition set up for later this year, so watch this space. There's lots coming, but I won't spill the beans just yet."

   a) Underline all the examples of alliteration in the text.
   What is the effect of the author's use of alliteration?

   b) i) What language technique is used in each of the following quotations?

   "Chai is an angel" ....

   "the paintings speak for themselves" ....

   "I won't spill the beans" ....

   ii) Explain the effect that each of these techniques has on the reader.

2. The extract below is from a soldier's diary entry.

   > I can hear voices outside that are scaring me half to death. I am engulfed by unrelenting dread and thoughts that the unspeakable will occur. This fear is tiresome, an incessant ache that I simply never escape from.
   >
   > I know I should remain as motionless as possible, but without my comrades I only have this pen for company. Writing down these thoughts is the only hope I have of stopping my hands from trembling. It never stops the ache though. No, it never stops the ache.

   a) Underline three examples of emotive language in the text.

   b) What is the effect of this emotive language on the reader? Explain your answer.

Language Techniques

3. Extracts A-D are from different texts.

A Still using the same archaic vacuum cleaner? Struggling to tidy those hard-to-reach areas? BOOM! We've invented a new state-of-the-art, cordless technology that will clean every corner of your house in deafening silence, shrinking automatically to fit in even the most awkward of spots. We make those stubborn spaces spotless.

B By now, the butter will be bubbling quietly. If it begins to hiss and splutter, reduce the heat. Combine the golden sugar with the lemon juice. The delectable fusion of tangy lemon and caramel tones will make the mix taste bittersweet.

C The city centre attracted a small crowd today when news spread that a bold black bear had been sighted near the cathedral. Self-proclaimed bear expert, Owen Paws, stated, "It's a definite possibility — black bears can be very sociable creatures."

D The band's new album can be labelled as nothing but a sparkling success after going platinum. The unlikely blend of jazz and rock influences makes for a sort of organised chaos, something which the band say was completely intentional.

a) i) Circle two language techniques below that are used in all four extracts.

| simile | oxymoron | personification | metaphor | alliteration |

ii) Underline the examples of these two techniques in each text.

b) i) What technique is used in the first two lines of text A? Explain its effect.

....

....

ii) Why do you think this technique isn't used in the other texts?

c) i) Find an example of descriptive language in text B.

....

ii) Why has the author included this particular technique in this type of text?

d) i) Which two texts use onomatopoeia?

....

ii) Why is this an effective technique in these text types?

Remember to think about each text's purpose.

 Look back at the different types of non-fiction texts over the last two pages. Pick one of them, and have a go at writing a similar text, but on a new topic. Think carefully about why certain language techniques are used in that text type, and try to include them in your writing too.

Section 2: Reading — Non-Fiction Texts © Not to be photocopied

Tone

The tone of a text is the mood the writer communicates. It's so fantastically, amazingly clever that writers can communicate an emotion just through the wondrous power of words, isn't it? Sorry, I'll tone it down.

1. The extract below is from a letter of complaint to an MP.

> As a constituent in your area, I am writing to express my utter disappointment regarding the plans released today for the number 75 bus route to be cut. Public transport has suffered excessive cuts in the last decade, and this is the last bus route that passes through my village. Living in such a rural area, many local residents rely on public services like these to get around. I do NOT feel that the decision to cut the route is representative of the constituents you serve. Have you really thought about the implications of this decision? You are cutting off a lifeline that so many of us rely on.
>
> Scrapping the only public transport route from our village into the city is likely to encourage more cars on the roads — an outrageous notion in the midst of a climate crisis. It is also certainly going to isolate older people living in our area, leading to yet more social exclusion and loneliness. I know my elderly neighbour was very distressed to hear about your decision.

a) i) Write down two adjectives that describe the tone of the extract.

....

ii) Write down evidence from the text to support your choice of words.

....

....

iii) How do the quotes you found build the desired tone?

iv) Why is this an effective tone for the letter's intended reader?

2. Have a look at the table below and answer the questions.

Text	Appropriate Tone
a fan letter	
a sympathy card	
an 'Agony Aunt' blog	
a food nutrition label	
a protest speech	
a diary entry	

passionate

candid

informative

complimentary

compassionate

advisory

a) Complete the table using the adjectives in the box. You can only use each word once.

b) Write down some example phrases for each text that would create the appropriate tone.

© Not to be photocopied   Section 2: Reading — Non-Fiction Texts

What You Think

It's valuable to be able to take things from the text and form your own opinions about them. The writer always has the reader in mind, so your perspective matters — just back up your ideas with evidence.

1. The extract below is from a travel blog.

   > It will be so hard to leave — I have truly fallen in love with this place. I'm going to miss the warmth of the fine golden sand around my feet and the gentle crash of the ocean's soft waves. I might even miss the intense pulse of fierce heat on my back as I stroll through the markets.
   >
   > This town breathes peace and serenity, and I feel almost awakened by the sleepiness of it all. Finally taking time out from the hectic disarray of normal life has renewed and restored me. There is something so appealing about visiting a place untouched by chaos — no preconceptions or expectations, just a charming place with an enchanting modesty about it. Next time you're thinking of taking some time out to go to the most popular tourist hotspot, consider going off-piste instead. Take the road less travelled. You can find such beauty in the unconventional and such freedom in being offbeat.

   a) How did the extract make you feel?

   ....

   ....

   b) i) How does the author use language to create a calming tone?

   ....

   ii) How does this tone appeal to the reader? Explain your answer.

   ....

   ....

   c) How does the author's tone shift in the last few sentences?
   Why do you think the author does this?

   d) Copy and complete the table, summarising the effect of each phrase on the reader.

Quote	Effect
"the intense pulse of fierce heat on my back"	
"This town breathes peace and serenity"	
"such freedom in being offbeat"	

   e) Do you think the purpose of the text has been achieved? Explain why or why not.

Section 2: Reading — Non-Fiction Texts

The Author's Intentions

Texts can be designed to express certain viewpoints and ideas. Close analysis of their language can help you come up with a theory on what these might be — you just have to follow the writer's breadcrumbs.

1. The extract below is from a speech protesting against animal testing.

> Countless animals are subjected to pain and physical suffering each year on account of outdated research techniques. The statistics are harrowing. It is thought that over 100 million animals experience this ill treatment across the globe. Every. Single. Year. Picture this — you're born into the world, only to be subjected to a life of suffering, crammed into a box, with any sense of freedom snatched from you.
>
> On top of this, you have absolutely no voice to even try to resist this fate — all you know is suffering. But here's the thing — science is now advanced enough to use more humane procedures, most of which are *much* more useful for understanding how products will work on humans. Today, animal suffering is nonsensical, needless and altogether barbaric. Our voices mean something, and if we shout loud enough, the people inflicting this pain will have to listen to us. If you truly care about animals, speak up. Together, we can throw a light on this issue, and in turn spread some hope for the animals enslaved by these practices.

a) Who is the author's intended audience?

....

b) What is the primary purpose of this text? Circle your answer.

| to inform | to entertain | to persuade | to advise |

c) How does the author use punctuation for effect in the first paragraph? Explain your answer.

....

....

d) Tick the statement that best explains why the author uses imagery.

It delivers the text's message quickly and also concisely. ☐

It forces the reader to imagine the animals' experiences. ☐

It creates a much more pleasurable reading experience. ☐

e) Sum up the author's tone using one adjective. Why have they used this tone?

f) Find two examples of emotive language in the text. Why has the author included them?

g) 'The author speaks authoritatively.'
Do you agree with this statement? Explain why or why not.

 Read through the extract again. Can you think of any arguments against animal testing that are not mentioned in the text? Write a few paragraphs of your own that outline these additional arguments, and use persuasive language techniques to convey your message effectively.

Section 3: Reading — Fiction and Plays

Congratulations, you have reached the next section. This time, it's the weird and wonderful world of make-believe. That's right, the home of all things character, plot, theme and setting. So grab a hot beverage of your choice and make yourself comfortable — boy, do I have a few stories to tell you...

Before you Start

1. Here is an adapted extract from *The Importance of Being Earnest* by Oscar Wilde. In the play, Jack creates an imaginary alter ego, Ernest, who Gwendolen falls for.

   > JACK [*nervously*]: Miss Fairfax, ever since I met you I have admired you more than any girl... I have ever met since... I met you.
   >
   > GWENDOLEN: Yes, I am quite well aware of the fact. For me you have always had an irresistible fascination. Even before I met you I was far from indifferent to you. [JACK *looks at her in amazement.*] My ideal has always been to love someone of the name of Ernest.
   >
   > JACK: But you don't really mean to say that you couldn't love me if my name wasn't Ernest?
   >
   > GWENDOLEN: But your name is Ernest.
   >
   > JACK: Personally, darling, to speak quite candidly, I don't much care about the name of Ernest... I don't think the name suits me at all.
   >
   > GWENDOLEN: It suits you perfectly. It is a divine name. It has a music of its own. It produces vibrations.
   >
   > JACK: Well, really, Gwendolen, I must say that I think there are lots of other much nicer names. I think Jack, for instance, a charming name.
   >
   > GWENDOLEN: Jack?... No, there is very little music in the name Jack, if any at all, indeed. It does not thrill. It produces absolutely no vibrations... I have known several Jacks, and they all, without exception, were more than usually plain. The only really safe name is Ernest.
   >
   > JACK: Gwendolen, I must get christened at once — I mean we must get married at once.

   a) Circle the word that best describes the extract.

   | romantic | tragic | amusing | tense | melancholy | gruesome |

   b) Find a quote to show that Gwendolen doesn't know something that the audience does.

   ....

   c) Describe how Gwendolen feels about the name Jack.
   Explain how the audience might respond to her feelings.

   ....

   ....

   d) Do you agree with the following statement: 'Gwendolen is a superficial character.'?
   Explain your answer using details from the extract.

Finding Evidence in the Text

As any good crime drama will show you, an idea without evidence is mere speculation. Examiners don't mind a theory as long as you support it with evidence, so always present your case with proof from the text.

1. The extract below is from the story *Rushing*.

> Lauren tapped her foot impatiently. She glanced at her watch and silently urged the train to reach her station. Curse that extra 15 minutes of sleep, she thought. The summer was taking its toll, and a bead of sweat trickled down her face. Still no air conditioning on these things...
>
> Sleeping in had meant she had missed the rush hour zombies, but she was now confronted with a whole new monster: dawdling sightseers. The train jerked to a halt and several lost their balance. She smirked, but was quickly engulfed by crowds of them as they vacated the train at her stop, carrying her through the station.
>
> Freeing herself from the swarm of tourists, she scaled the escalator in unflinching strides, the clock ticking, beating, pounding in her head.
>
> Outside, she weaved in and out of the market crowds like a needle pulling thread. The smell of freshly baked bread floated through the air and her belly groaned.
>
> There it was, her journey's end. Swiftly, she slipped behind the market stall. She tied her apron as best as she could with trembling hands. Had she done it?
>
> "Late again," a voice said.

a) Why is Lauren running late?

....

b) Find a quote from the text that shows that Lauren is...

stressed: ....

hot: ....

nervous: ....

agile: ....

c) i) What are the people Lauren encounters in the station compared to?

ii) What does this imagery suggest about Lauren's attitude to the people she encounters? Explain your answer.

d) Would you describe Lauren as a conscientious character? Explain your answer using evidence from the text.

 Now it's time to practise using evidence to build a great argument. Answer this question about the extract above: 'How does the writer create a sense of tension?' Write some paragraphs that each make a point. Back everything up with evidence, and explain how it supports each point.

Making Inferences

Unfortunately, writers don't always make it easy for you — sometimes, you have to work some of the details out for yourself. I like to think of it as deciphering a code, but you might prefer reading between the lines.

1. The extract below is from *The Humans* by Matt Haig.

> So, what is this?
>
> You ready?
>
> Okay. Inhale. I will tell you.
>
> This book, this actual book, is set right *here*, on Earth. It is about the meaning of life and nothing at all. It is about what it takes to kill somebody, and save them. It is about love and dead poets and wholenut peanut butter. It's about matter and anti-matter, everything and nothing, hope and hate. It's about a forty-one-year-old female historian called Isobel and her fifteen-year-old son called Gulliver and the cleverest mathematician in the world. It is, in short, about how to become a human.
>
> But let me state the obvious. I was not one. That first night, in the cold and the dark and the wind, I was nowhere near. Before I read *Cosmopolitan*, in the garage, I had never even seen this written language. I realise that this could be your first time too. To give you an idea of the way people here consume stories, I have put this book together as a human would. The words I use are human words, typed in a human font, laid out consecutively in the human style. With your almost instantaneous ability to translate even the most exotic and primitive linguistic forms, I trust comprehension should not be a problem.

a) Pick out a word or phrase which suggests that the narrator has an unusual story to tell.

....

b) Copy and complete the table by making an inference from each quote from the extract.

Quote from the extract	Inference
"This book, this actual book, is set right *here*, on Earth."	
"It is, in short, about how to become a human."	

c) i) Who do you think the narrator is addressing in this extract?

....

ii) Explain your answer to part i), using evidence from the text.

d) i) What impression does the narrator give of what it means to be human? Use evidence from the text to explain your answer.

ii) Do you think the narrator likes humans? Explain your answer.

Structure

We all need a bit of structure in our lives, and fiction is no different. Authors structure their texts in different ways depending on their intentions. You need to try and work out what the effect of this structure might be.

1. The extract below is from the story *A Little Differently*.

   > Let me tell you something about me. I see the world a little differently to everyone else.
   > *You can say that again.*
   > Stop it. You're making me lose my train of thought.
   > *What? I am your thoughts.*
   > You know what I mean. Anyway. My life is a little different to the average person's. If there's such a thing as an 'average' person. I'm sure we all have our quirks. One of yours might be that you know exactly what I'm going to say. Was I right? Do you?
   > *Of course they don't. Just get on with it.*
   > Please be quiet. You're showing yourself up. You're showing *us* up. OK, I will explain. I see the world a little differently to everyone else. I suppose I see it... repeatedly? I see the world a little differently... because I've lived this very same day for 22 years.
   > *With only me for company.*

   a) Write down a phrase that is repeated in this extract. Explain the effect of this repetition.

   ....

   ....

   ....

   b) Who is the narrator in the lines in italics?

   ....

   c) i) How does the author use structure to show that the text has two narrators?

   ....

   ....

   ii) Do you think this structure is effective? Explain your answer.

   d) How does the author use structure to create humour in this extract?
      Explain your answer using evidence from the text.

   e) What impression of the narrator does this extract create?
      Explain how the author uses structure to create this impression.

 Since you now know the structure of this extract like the back of your hand (we go way back, my hand and I), have a go at continuing the extract, using the structural devices that the author has used. Write three paragraphs, making sure you think about the effect of each structural device.

© Not to be photocopied Section 3: Reading — Fiction and Plays

Themes

Themes are those really important ideas in a text that you just can't get away from. Picking up on them is a true love of mine, which is fitting actually, because I think you could say 'love is in the air' in the texts below.

1. The text below is an abridged extract from *David Copperfield* by Charles Dickens. In this extract, the narrator, David, reflects on his feelings for Dora.

    > I was a captive and a slave. I loved Dora Spenlow to distraction!
    >
    > She was more than human to me. She was a Fairy, I don't know what she was — anything that no one ever saw, and everything that everybody ever wanted. I was swallowed up in an abyss of love in an instant. There was no pausing on the brink; no looking down, or looking back; I was gone, headlong, before I had sense to say a word to her.

    a) Write down a quote that suggests that David has no choice but to love Dora.

    ....

    b) David falls "headlong" into an "abyss of love". What does this suggest about David's love?

    c) i) What impression of love do you get from the extract? Tick one option.

    Love can be confusing. ☐   Love can be all-consuming. ☐

    Love can be ordinary. ☐   Love can take time to develop. ☐

    ii) Using examples from the text, explain how Dickens creates this impression.

2. The text below is an abridged extract from *Jane Eyre* by Charlotte Brontë. In this extract, Rochester professes his love for Jane, who is employed as a governess for his daughter.

    > "Every atom of your flesh is as dear to me as my own: in pain and sickness it would still be dear. Your mind is my treasure, and if it were broken, it would be my treasure still. If you flew at me wildly, I should receive you in an embrace. I should not shrink from you with disgust: in your quiet moments you should have no watcher and no nurse but me; and I could hang over you with untiring tenderness, though you gave me no smile in return; and never weary of gazing into your eyes, though they had no longer a ray of recognition for me."

    a) What does Rochester's use of the word "treasure" suggest about his feelings for Jane?

    ....

    b) How does Brontë show that love can be difficult? Explain your answer.

3. Read both extracts again. Using examples from the extracts, explain the similarities and differences between David's love for Dora and Rochester's love for Jane.

Section 3: Reading — Fiction and Plays

Language Techniques

By now you've probably got pretty good at spotting language techniques, but you also need to analyse the effect of those techniques. Every time you see one, try to think about what purpose it's serving in the text.

1. The extract below is from *Romeo and Juliet* by William Shakespeare.

   > ROMEO: But soft, what light through yonder window breaks?
   > It is the east, and Juliet is the sun.
   > Arise, fair sun, and kill the envious moon,
   > Who is already sick and pale with grief
   > That thou, her maid, art far more fair than she.
   > Be not her maid, since she is envious,
   > Her vestal livery* is but sick and green,
   > And none but fools do wear it; cast it off.
   >
   > JULIET *appears above at a window*
   >
   > It is my lady, O it is my love!
   > O that she knew she were!
   > She speaks, yet she says nothing; what of that?
   > Her eye discourses, I will answer it.
   > I am too bold, 'tis not to me she speaks.
   > Two of the fairest stars in all the heaven,
   > Having some business, do entreat her eyes
   > To twinkle in their spheres till they return.
   > What if her eyes were there, they in her head?
   > The brightness of her cheek would shame those stars,
   > As daylight doth a lamp.

   *vestal livery — clothing worn by a virgin

   a) i) Write down an example of a rhetorical question from this extract.

   ....

   ii) Explain the effect of Shakespeare's use of rhetorical questions throughout this extract.

   b) i) Write down two examples of personification in the first half of the extract.

   ....

   ....

   ii) What is the effect of this personification? Explain your answer.

   c) Explain how Shakespeare uses figurative language in the first half of the extract to emphasise Romeo's admiration for Juliet. Support your answer with quotations.

   d) How does Shakespeare use imagery to emphasise Juliet's beauty after she appears at the window? Support your answer using evidence from the extract.

What's that? You want to spend more time thinking about this extract? Well, luckily for you I've got a fantastic task in mind — write a character description of Juliet in prose, from Romeo's point of view. Use descriptive language and the techniques covered on this page. And... go!

© Not to be photocopied   Section 3: Reading — Fiction and Plays

Characterisation

Stories would be pretty boring without their characters. Always remember that authors make characters the way they are for a reason — sussing out what makes them tick can tell you a lot more about the text.

1. This extract is from *Pan's Labyrinth: The Labyrinth of the Faun* by Guillermo del Toro and Cornelia Funke.

   > Her name was Ofelia and she knew everything about the pain of loss, although she was only thirteen years old. Her father had died just a year ago and Ofelia missed him so terribly that at times her heart felt like an empty box with nothing but the echo of her pain in it. She often wondered whether her mother felt the same, but she couldn't find the answer in her pale face.
   >
   > "As white as snow, as red as blood, as black as coal," Ofelia's father used to say when he looked at her mother, his voice soft with tenderness. "You look so much like her, Ofelia." Lost.
   >
   > They had been driving for hours, farther and farther away from everything Ofelia knew, deeper and deeper into this never-ending forest, to meet the man her mother had chosen to be Ofelia's new father. Ofelia called him the Wolf, and she didn't want to think about him. But even the trees seemed to whisper his name.
   >
   > The only piece of home Ofelia had been able to take with her were some of her books. She closed her fingers firmly around the one on her lap, caressing the cover. When she opened the book, the white pages were so bright against the shadows that filled the forest and the words they offered granted shelter and comfort. The letters were like footprints in the snow, a wide white landscape untouched by pain, unharmed by memories too dark to keep, too sweet to let go of.
   >
   > "Why did you bring all these books, Ofelia? We'll be in the country!" The car ride had paled her mother's face even more. The car ride and the baby she was carrying. She grabbed the book from Ofelia's hands and all the comforting words fell silent.
   >
   > "You are too old for fairy tales, Ofelia! You need to start looking at the world!"
   >
   > Her mother's voice was like a broken bell. Ofelia couldn't remember her ever sounding like that when her father was still alive.

   a) Circle the correct option to complete each sentence.
   Find an example from the text to back up each of your choices.

   i) Ofelia's father seems **hopeful** / **warm** in the extract.

   ii) Ofelia uses books to **escape from** / **help understand** her life.

   b) Write down a quote that shows that Ofelia feels negatively towards her stepfather.

   ....

   c) The writer uses the simile "Her mother's voice was like a broken bell".
   What does it suggest about Ofelia's mother?

   d) How does the writer make Ofelia seem isolated? Explain your answer.

   e) 'Ofelia seems like a defeated character.' Do you agree with this statement?
   Explain your answer using examples from the extract.

Section 3: Reading — Fiction and Plays

Characterisation

2. The extract below is from the play *A Raisin in the Sun* by Lorraine Hansberry.

> **Travis** (*eating*)   This is the morning we supposed to bring the fifty cents to school.
> **Ruth**   Well, I ain't got no fifty cents this morning.
> **Travis**   Teacher say we have to.
> **Ruth**   I don't care what teacher say. I ain't got it. Eat your breakfast, Travis.
> **Travis**   I *am* eating.
> **Ruth**   Hush up now and just eat!
> *The boy gives her an exasperated look for her lack of understanding, and eats grudgingly.*
> **Travis**   You think Grandmama would have it?
> **Ruth**   No! And I want you to stop asking your grandmother for money, you hear me?
> **Travis** (*outraged*)   Gaaaleee! I don't ask her, she just gimme it sometimes!
> **Ruth**   Travis Willard Younger — I got too much on me this morning to be —
> **Travis**   Maybe Daddy —
> **Ruth**   Travis!
> *The boy hushes abruptly. They are both quiet and tense for several seconds.*
> **Travis** (*presently*)   Could I maybe go carry some groceries in front of the supermarket for a little while after school then?
> **Ruth**   Just hush, I said. (**Travis** *jabs his spoon into his cereal bowl viciously, and rests his head in anger upon his fists.*) If you through eating, you can get over there and make up your bed.
> *The boy obeys stiffly and crosses the room, almost mechanically, to the bed and more or less carefully folds the covering. He carries the bedding into his mother's room and returns with his books and cap.*
> **Travis** (*sulking and standing apart from her unnaturally*)   I'm gone.
> **Ruth** (*looking up from the stove to inspect him automatically*)   Come here. (*He crosses to her and she studies his head.*) If you don't take this comb and fix this here head, you better! (**Travis** *puts down his books with a great sigh of oppression, and crosses to the mirror. His mother mutters under her breath about his 'stubbornness'.*) 'Bout to march out of here with that head looking just like chickens slept in it! I just don't know where you get your stubborn ways . . . And get your jacket, too. Looks chilly out this morning.
> **Travis** (*with conspicuously brushed hair and jacket*)   I'm gone.

a) Which word best describes how Travis is feeling? Find a quote that supports your answer.

sociable ☐   frustrated ☐   despairing ☐   nonchalant ☐

b) Would you describe Travis as determined? Explain your answer.

....

....

c) Look at the way Ruth speaks to Travis. How can you tell that she's assertive towards him?

d) Do you think Ruth and Travis are similar characters? Use evidence to support your answer.

Setting

Settings provide the backdrop for a story — they help shape the text's atmosphere and can also give handy hints about what's going on. So take note of everything, from the location down to the colour of leaves.

1. The abridged extract below is from *The Hound of the Baskervilles* by Arthur Conan Doyle.

   > We had left the fertile country behind and beneath us. We looked back on it now, the slanting rays of a low sun turning the streams to threads of gold and glowing on the red earth new turned by the plough and the broad tangle of the woodlands. The road in front of us grew bleaker and wilder over huge russet and olive slopes, sprinkled with giant boulders. Now and then we passed a moorland cottage, walled and roofed with stone, with no creeper to break its harsh outline. Suddenly we looked down into a cuplike depression, patched with stunted oaks and firs which had been twisted and bent by the fury of years of storm. Two high, narrow towers rose over the trees. The driver pointed with his whip.
   >
   > "Baskerville Hall," said he.
   >
   > Its master had risen and was staring with flushed cheeks and shining eyes. A few minutes later we had reached the lodge-gates, a maze of fantastic tracery in wrought iron, with weather-bitten pillars on either side, blotched with lichens, and surmounted by the boars' heads of the Baskervilles. The lodge was a ruin of black granite and bared ribs of rafters, but facing it was a new building, half constructed.
   >
   > Through the gateway we passed into the avenue, where the wheels were again hushed amid the leaves, and the old trees shot their branches in a sombre tunnel over our heads. Baskerville shuddered as he looked up the long, dark drive to where the house glimmered like a ghost at the farther end.

   I'm glimmering! I look incredible... Thanks Arthur.

   a) Find evidence from the text to support each of the statements below.

   i) Baskerville Hall was grand and ornate.

   ....

   ii) Part of the Baskerville Hall estate is dilapidated.

   ....

   b) How does the author use colours in the extract to suggest a change in atmosphere? Explain your answer using evidence from the text.

   c) The author describes how Baskerville Hall "glimmered like a ghost". What impression of the hall does this create? Explain your answer.

   d) i) Tick the adjective that best describes the atmosphere in this extract.

   terrifying ☐   vibrant ☐   bustling ☐   unsettling ☐   ordinary ☐

   ii) How does the author use descriptions of nature to build this atmosphere?

Section 3: Reading — Fiction and Plays

Setting

2. The extracts below are from *The Book Thief* by Markus Zusak. They are narrated by Death, who comes to collect souls after a bombing of a German town during World War Two.

> The sky was like soup, boiling and stirring. In some places it was burned. There were black crumbs, and pepper, streaked amongst the redness.
>   Earlier, kids had been playing hopscotch there, on the street that looked like oil-stained pages. When I arrived I could still hear the echoes. The feet tapping the road. The children-voices laughing, and the smiles like salt, but decaying fast.
>   Then, bombs.
>
> This time, everything was too late.
>   The sirens. The cuckoo shrieks in the radio. All too late.
>
> Within minutes, mounds of concrete and earth were stacked and piled. The streets were ruptured veins. Blood streamed till it was dried on the road, and the bodies were stuck there, like driftwood after the flood.

a) How does the author create a threatening atmosphere at the start of the extract? Refer to language in your answer.

....

....

b) The author describes the sound of "laughing" being replaced with "shrieks" and "sirens". What effect does this have on the reader?

....

....

c) What device is used in "The streets were ruptured veins"? Why do you think the author has described the streets in this way? Explain your answer.

d) How does the atmosphere in the extract below differ from that in the extract above? Use examples from the text to support your answer.

> For hours, the sky remained a devastating, home-cooked red. The small German town had been flung apart one more time. Snowflakes of ash fell so *lovelily* you were tempted to stretch out your tongue to catch them, taste them. Only, they would have scorched your lips. They would have cooked your mouth.

This extract is taken from slightly later on in The Book Thief and describes the aftermath of the event in the previous extract.

 Now have a go at writing your own detailed description of a setting. You could set your story in a remote country house, a war-torn town, or somewhere completely different. Make sure the language you use in your description creates an appropriate atmosphere for the setting.

Interpreting Plays

Playwrights tend to keep descriptions brief, so you've got to work out what's going on in other ways. Make sure you look at dialogue and stage directions — the way the actors move and speak can reveal a lot.

1. The extract below is from *The Crucible* by Arthur Miller. In this scene, Mary Warren claims she, along with the other girls, has been pretending to see spirits so they could falsely accuse people of practising witchcraft.

   > MARY WARREN: It's not a trick! *She stands.* I—I used to faint because I—I thought I saw spirits.
   >
   > DANFORTH: *Thought* you saw them!
   >
   > MARY WARREN: But I did not, Your Honor.
   >
   > HATHORNE: How could you think you saw them unless you saw them?
   >
   > *This play is based on the Salem witch trials which took place in 1692-93. These trials began when a group of young girls claimed to have been bewitched by locals, accusing many people of witchcraft.*
   >
   > MARY WARREN: I—I cannot tell how, but I did. I—I heard the other girls screaming, and you, Your Honor, you seemed to believe them, and I— It were only sport in the beginning, sir, but then the whole world cried spirits, spirits, and I—I promise you, Mr. Danforth, I only thought I saw them but I did not.
   >
   > *Danforth peers at her.*
   >
   > PARRIS, *smiling, but nervous because Danforth seems to be struck by Mary Warren's story*: Surely Your Excellency is not taken by this simple lie.
   >
   > DANFORTH, *turning worriedly to Abigail*: Abigail. I bid you now search your heart and tell me this—and beware of it, child, to God every soul is precious and His vengeance is terrible on them that take life without cause. Is it possible, child, that the spirits you have seen are illusion only, some deception that may cross your mind when—
   >
   > ABIGAIL: Why, this—this—is a base question, sir.
   >
   > DANFORTH: Child, I would have you consider it—
   >
   > ABIGAIL: I have been hurt, Mr Danforth; I have seen my blood runnin' out! I have been near to murdered every day because I done my duty pointing out the Devil's people—and this is my reward? To be mistrusted, denied, questioned like a—
   >
   > DANFORTH, *weakening*: Child, I do not mistrust you—
   >
   > ABIGAIL, *in an open threat*: Let *you* beware, Mr. Danforth. Think you to be so mighty that the power of Hell may not turn *your* wits? Beware of it! There is— *Suddenly, from an accusatory attitude, her face turns, looking into the air above—it is truly frightened.*
   >
   > DANFORTH, *apprehensively*: What is it, child?
   >
   > ABIGAIL, *looking about in the air, clasping her arms about her as though cold*: I—I know not. A wind, a cold wind, has come.
   >
   > *Her eyes fall on Mary Warren.*
   >
   > MARY WARREN, *terrified, pleading*: Abby!
   >
   > MERCY LEWIS, *shivering*: Your Honor, I freeze!
   >
   > PROCTOR: They're pretending!

   a) How does Abigail feel when she says "I have been hurt"? Why does she feel this way?

   ....

   ....

Interpreting Plays

b) Number the events below 1-5 so they are in the correct order.

○ Danforth asks Abigail if she definitely saw spirits.

○ Parris doubts Mary's claim and tries to influence Danforth.

○ Mary admits she didn't see spirits.

○ Abigail and Mercy seem to experience something supernatural.

○ Abigail threatens Danforth.

A witch? Me? No chance! I just erm... really like sweeping...

c) Write out a quote from the extract that backs up each point below.

   i) Parris is less powerful than Danforth.

   ....

   ii) Danforth is a religious man.

   ....

d) The playwright includes lots of hesitation in Mary's dialogue. What does this suggest?

   ....
   ....

e) Describe how the atmosphere changes throughout the extract.

   ....
   ....
   ....

f) Do you think that Danforth believes Mary? Explain your answer.

g) How does the playwright use structure to make the extract dramatic? Explain your answer.

h) 'Abigail is a manipulative character.' Do you agree with this statement? Explain your answer using details from the extract.

i) Do you think that Abigail and Mercy are pretending at the end of the extract? Explain your answer using evidence from the text.

© Not to be photocopied   Section 3: Reading — Fiction and Plays

Staging and Performance

At this stage in your literary career, you've probably read a few plays, but don't forget that they're written to be performed. Think about how a script can be communicated on stage, props and all — break a leg.

1. This extract is from *Macbeth* by William Shakespeare.

    > MACBETH: Is this a dagger which I see before me,
    > The handle toward my hand? Come, let me clutch thee.
    > I have thee not, and yet I see thee still.
    > Art thou not, fatal vision, sensible
    > To feeling as to sight? Or art thou but
    > A dagger of the mind, a false creation,
    > Proceeding from the heat-oppressèd brain?
    > I see thee yet, in form as palpable
    > As this which now I draw.
    > Thou marshall'st me the way that I was going,
    > And such an instrument I was to use.
    > Mine eyes are made the fools o' the other senses,
    > Or else worth all the rest. I see thee still,
    > And on thy blade and dudgeon gouts of blood,
    > Which was not so before. There's no such thing:
    > It is the bloody business which informs
    > Thus to mine eyes.

    *dudgeon — the handle of a dagger

    a) Summarise how Macbeth's thoughts and feelings change throughout this extract.

    b) i) For each of the quotations in the table, suggest how the actor playing Macbeth could speak and move to help the audience understand Macbeth's thoughts during his speech.

Quotation	How could the actor speak and move?
"Is this a dagger which I see before me"	
"Come, let me clutch thee. / I have thee not"	
"on thy blade and dudgeon gouts of blood"	

    Analyse each quotation, then think about how staging and performance could be used to help convey meaning.

    ii) Explain why you made each of your staging suggestions for the quotations in the table.

    c) How would you stage the dagger's presence? Do you think that the audience should be able to see the dagger, or should only Macbeth to be able to see it? Explain your answer.

 Is this a pen which I see before me, the handle toward my hand? Ahem. Rewrite the extract above, adding in stage directions to guide an actor playing Macbeth. Use your answers above to help you. Think about how the actor should speak and move when saying the lines.

Section 3: Reading — Fiction and Plays © Not to be photocopied

What You Think

Writers will guide how you feel about characters and events, but you'll probably find you still develop your own thoughts about them. Sink your teeth into the extract below — let's see what you think...

1. The adapted extract below is from *Dracula* by Bram Stoker.

> I heard a heavy step approaching behind the great door, and saw through the chinks the gleam of a coming light. Then there was the sound of rattling chains and the clanking of massive bolts drawn back. A key was turned with the loud grating noise of long disuse, and the great door swung back.
>
> Within, stood a tall old man, clean shaven save for a long white moustache, and clad in black from head to foot, without a single speck of colour about him anywhere. He held in his hand an antique silver lamp, which threw long quivering shadows as it flickered in the draught of the open door. The old man motioned me in with a courtly gesture, saying in excellent English, but with a strange intonation: —
>
> "Welcome to my house! Enter freely and of your own will!" He made no motion of stepping to meet me, but stood like a statue, as though his gesture of welcome had fixed him into stone. The instant, however, that I had stepped over the threshold, he moved impulsively forward, and holding out his hand grasped mine with a strength which made me wince, an effect which was not lessened by the fact that it seemed as cold as ice — more like the hand of a dead than a living man.

a) i) Circle the word you think best describes how the narrator feels in this extract.

| annoyed | curious | comfortable | petrified | fascinated |

ii) Do you find his reaction surprising? Explain your answer.

....

....

b) Why do you think the author focuses on sound in the first paragraph? Explain your answer.

....

....

c) The old man tells the narrator "Enter freely and of your own will!"
How does this greeting make you feel? Explain your answer.

....

....

d) What effect does the setting of the extract have on the reader? Explain your answer.

e) How does the description of the old man make you feel?
Explain your answer using evidence from the extract.

© Not to be photocopied   Section 3: Reading — Fiction and Plays

Section 4: Reading — Poetry

Ah, poetry... it's so fantastic that this entire section is dedicated to it — that's right, nine whole pages of poetic goodness for you to get all lyrical about! From techniques to rhyme schemes, voice to themes, this section really does have it all. By the end, I guarantee that you'll be a lyrical legend...*

*This cannot be guaranteed, but you'll probably be a bit better at reading poetry.

Before you Start

1. The poem below is 'What If This Road' by Sheenagh Pugh.

What if this road, that has held no surprises
these many years, decided not to go
home after all; what if it could turn
left or right with no more ado
than a kite-tail? What if its tarry* skin
were like a long, supple bolt of cloth*,
that is shaken and rolled out, and takes
a new shape from the contours beneath?
And if it chose to lay itself down
in a new way, around a blind corner,
across hills you must climb without knowing
what's on the other side, who would not hanker*
to be going, at all risks? Who wants to know
a story's end, or where a road will go?

*tarry — containing tar

*bolt of cloth — a wide, rolled-up length of cloth

*hanker — want very much

a) i) What do you think the road in the poem is an extended metaphor for? Tick one box.

a book ☐   the narrator's upcoming trip ☐   life ☐

ii) Explain your answer to part i), using evidence from the poem.

b) Why do you think the poet uses rhetorical questions in the poem?

....

....

c) Why does the poet compare the road to "a long, supple bolt of cloth"?

....

....

d) Summarise what you think the poet's message is in the last rhetorical question.

....

....

Making Inferences

When you read a poem, you need to make sure you're not just well-versed in what happens in the text — you've also got to work out all the sneaky things that the poet merely hints at throughout the poem.

1. The poem below is 'The Long Hill' by Sara Teasdale.

    > I must have passed the crest a while ago
    >   And now I am going down.
    > Strange to have crossed the crest and not to know—
    >   But the brambles were always catching the hem of my gown.
    >
    > All the morning I thought how proud it would be
    >   To stand there straight as a queen—
    > Wrapped in the wind and the sun, with the world under me.
    >   But the air was dull, there was little I could have seen.
    >
    > It was nearly level along the beaten track
    >   And the brambles caught in my gown—
    > But it's no use now to think of turning back,
    >   The rest of the way will be only going down.

    a) What does the narrator compare life to throughout the poem? Circle one option.

    | royalty | the air | a hill | a gown |

    b) What do you think the poet means by the line "Strange to have crossed the crest and not to know"? Explain your answer.

    ....

    ....

    c) How do you think the narrator feels in the second stanza? Explain your answer.

    ....

    ....

    d) What do you think "the brambles" symbolise in the poem?

    ....

    e) What does Teasdale mean in the final line of the poem? Explain your answer.

Can't get enough of these poems? Well, you're in luck. Read 'What If This Road' (p.30) and 'The Long Hill' again. Then, write two paragraphs comparing the poems — think about the similarities and differences in each poem's message and how the poet presents their ideas.

Structure

Aha, you've struck structure — this is all to do with the way that ideas are arranged in a piece of writing. For next level answers, make sure you think about how a poem's structure reflects or relates to its content.

1. The poem below is 'Praise Song for My Mother' by Grace Nichols.

   > You were
   > water to me
   > deep and bold and fathoming
   >
   > You were
   > moon's eye to me
   > pull and grained and mantling*
   >
   > You were
   > sunrise to me
   > rise and warm and streaming
   >
   > You were
   > the fish's red gill to me
   > the flame tree's spread to me
   > the crab's leg/the fried plantain smell replenishing replenishing
   >
   > Go to your wide futures, you said

   A praise song is a traditional African form which celebrates the qualities of something.

   *mantling — enveloping or covering

   a) i) What is the form of the poem? Circle one option.

      | elegy | ballad | free verse | hymn | blank verse |

      ii) Why do you think the poet chose to use this form for the poem?

      ....

      ....

   b) The poem doesn't use much punctuation. Why do you think the poet has done this?

      ....

      ....

   c) Explain why the poet uses lots of repetition, using at least two examples from the poem.

   d) Describe the stanza and line lengths in the first four stanzas. What is their effect?

      ....

      ....

   e) The final line of the poem is in a stanza of its own.
      Explain why you think the poet has done this.

Section 4: Reading — Poetry

Themes

It's not just stories that have themes — poems have them too. Just like stories, some of the most common themes in poetry are love and home. (That might be a tiny hint about the themes of the poem below...)

1. The poem below is 'The City of my birth' by Karl Nova.

Karl Nova is a hip hop artist, poet and author.

> I spy with my London eye
> Big Ben telling the time
> as these thoughts like the River Thames
> flow through my mind
> Thoughts of love for my city
> Like tube trains move quickly
> Although unlike them
> there's no delay, swiftly
> like red buses that move through the streets
> Like the blood pumping through my veins
> as my heart beats
> I feel a rush of blood for the city of my birth
> I might be biased, it's one of the greatest on earth
> I stand still on Westminster bridge watching the movement
> of different people moving around I am grooving
> to music pumping in my headphones, I crack a smile
> London is my playground and I am its child.

Westminster Bridge is a famous bridge in London.

a) What does the phrase "rush of blood" tell you about the narrator's feelings for London?

....

b) The narrator compares their thoughts to "the River Thames", "tube trains" and "red buses". What do these similes suggest about the narrator's identity?

....

....

c) i) Nova uses little punctuation throughout the poem. What is the effect of this?

   It makes the poem sound choppy. ☐   It makes the poem flow steadily. ☐

   It brings the poem to abrupt stops. ☐   It makes the poem difficult to read. ☐

   ii) How does your answer to part i) help reflect the central theme of the poem?

   ....

   ....

d) What does the final phrase of the poem, "I am its child", suggest about the narrator's love for London? Explain your answer.

© Not to be photocopied

Section 4: Reading — Poetry

Voice

The voice of a poem is the person narrating it. How the narrator speaks and what words they use tell you a lot about their character — e.g. in this book I speak informally, which suggests I'm friendly (promise).

1. The poem below is 'To Travel This Ship' by James Berry.

> To travel this ship, man
> I gladly strip mi name
> of a one-cow, two-goat an a boar pig
> an sell the land piece mi father lef
> to be on this ship and to be a debtor.
> Man, jus fa diffrun days
> I woulda sell, borrow or thief
> jus fa diffrun sunrise an sundown
> in annodda place wid odda ways.
> To travel this ship, man
> I woulda hurt, I woulda cheat or lie,
> I strip mi yard, mi friend and cousin-them To get this yah ship ride.
> Man – I woulda sell mi modda Jus hopin to buy her back.
> Down in dat hole I was
> I see this lickle luck, man,
> I see this lickle light.
> Man, Jamaica is a place
> Where generations them start out Havin notn, earnin notn,
> And – dead – leavin notn.
> I did wake up every mornin and find notn change.
> Children them shame to go to school barefoot.
> Only a penny to buy lunch.
> Man, I have follow this lickle light for change.
> I a-follow it, man!

James Berry emigrated from Jamaica to Britain in 1948 as part of the Windrush generation. This poem is about the journey.

The ticket costs how much?!

a) i) Write down three examples of phonetic spelling from the poem.

....

ii) What do these spellings suggest about the narrator? Think about the poem's context.

....

....

b) i) In your own words, describe the tone of the poem.

....

ii) Explain your answer to part i). Support your explanation with quotes.

iii) What does the poem's tone suggest about the character of the narrator?

c) The poem is about the narrator's desire to leave Jamaica. Do you think they want to leave their heritage completely? Explain your answer, thinking about the poet's use of voice.

Section 4: Reading — Poetry © Not to be photocopied

Techniques

I feel like my life has been leading up to this point, and now it's here — a whole page about <u>cats</u>. It's also about the techniques the poet uses, such as figurative language, but it's mainly about cats.

1. The extract below is from 'Cats' by A.S.J. Tessimond.

    > Cats, no less liquid than their shadows,
    >   Offer no angles to the wind.
    > They slip, diminished, neat, through loopholes
    >   Less than themselves; will not be pinned
    >
    > To rules or routes for journeys; counter
    >   Attack with non-resistance; twist
    > Enticing through the curving fingers
    >   And leave an angered, empty fist.
    >
    > They wait, obsequious* as darkness —
    >   Quick to retire, quick to return;
    > Admit no aim or ethics; flatter
    >   With reservations; will not learn
    >
    > To answer to their names; are seldom
    >   Truly owned till shot and skinned.
    > Cats, no less liquid than their shadows,
    >   Offer no angles to the wind.

    *obsequious — obedient

    a) i) What does the description "no less liquid than their shadows" suggest about cats?

    ....

    ii) How does the poet's use of enjambment reflect this quality?

    ....

    ....

    Enjambment is when a phrase runs from one line or stanza to the next without punctuation.

    b) Write down a simile from the extract. What does this simile suggest about cats?

    ....

    ....

    ....

    c) The poet uses negative phrasing such as "no less", "will not" and "non-" in this extract. What do you think is the effect of this? Explain your answer.

    d) Explain how the poet uses language throughout the extract to capture the qualities of cats.

 Have a go at writing your own poem about an animal, which captures that animal's qualities. Use the techniques on this page, as well as other techniques you've studied, like personification, alliteration and onomatopoeia. Think carefully about the effect of each technique that you use.

© Not to be photocopied   Section 4: Reading — Poetry

Interpreting Poems

When you're interpreting a poem you've never seen before, read it over a few times to get a feel for the main ideas and themes. Then dive into the poem in more detail by looking at language and techniques.

1. The poem below is 'Patrolling Barnegat' by Walt Whitman.

   > Wild, wild the storm, and the sea high running,
   > Steady the roar of the gale, with incessant undertone muttering,
   > Shouts of demoniac laughter fitfully piercing and pealing,
   > Waves, air, midnight, their savagest trinity* lashing,
   > Out in the shadows there milk-white combs* careering,
   > On beachy slush and sand spirts of snow fierce slanting,
   > Where through the murk the easterly death-wind breasting,
   > Through cutting swirl and spray watchful and firm advancing,
   > (That in the distance! is that a wreck? is the red signal flaring?)
   >
   > Slush and sand of the beach tireless till daylight wending,
   > Steadily, slowly, through hoarse roar never remitting,
   > Along the midnight edge by those milk-white combs careering,
   > A group of dim, weird forms, struggling, the night confronting,
   > That savage trinity* warily watching.

   Barnegat is a place on the Atlantic Coast of the USA.

   *trinity — a group of three things
   *combs — waves

   a) Briefly summarise what the poem is about.

   ....

   b) Who do you think are the "group of dim, weird forms" described in the penultimate line?

   ....

   c) The poem uses lots of sibilance. Underline all the instances of sibilance you can find in the poem, then write down one example and explain its effect.

   ....
   ....
   ....

   Sibilance is the repetition of 's' and 'sh' sounds in words that are close together.

   d) i) Describe how rhythm is used in the poem.

   ....
   ....

   Rhythm is the pattern of sounds created by arranging stressed and unstressed syllables together.

   ii) Why do you think the poet uses rhythm in this way?

   e) The main theme of this poem is nature. What impression of nature is created? Back up your points using quotes from the poem.

   f) Briefly describe the tone of the poem. What effect does the tone have on the reader?

Section 4: Reading — Poetry

Interpreting Poems

2. The poem below is 'Ashes of Life' by Edna St. Vincent Millay.

> Love has gone and left me and the days are all alike;
> Eat I must, and sleep I will, — and would* that night were here!
> But ah! — to lie awake and hear the slow hours strike!
> Would* that it were day again! — with twilight near!
>
> Love has gone and left me and I don't know what to do;
> This or that or what you will is all the same to me;
> But all the things that I begin I leave before I'm through, —
> There's little use in anything as far as I can see.
>
> Love has gone and left me, — and the neighbours knock and borrow,
> And life goes on forever like the gnawing of a mouse, —
> And to-morrow and to-morrow and to-morrow and to-morrow
> There's this little street and this little house.

*would — wish

a) Tick the box next to the sentence that best summarises the first two stanzas of the poem.

The narrator finds relief from their misery by focusing on tasks and chores. ☐

The narrator's misery is making it difficult for them to complete daily tasks. ☐

Monotonous daily tasks have made the narrator feel miserable about life. ☐

b) i) Using evidence from the poem, describe how punctuation is used in the first stanza.

....

....

ii) What do you think this suggests about the narrator's feelings?

....

c) How does the poet use repetition in the poem? Explain your answer.

....

....

d) "And life goes on forever like the gnawing of a mouse".
Explain what Millay means in this line.

e) Read the last two lines of the poem. How does the narrator feel about their future? Explain your answer using evidence from the poem.

Go back to p.34 and reread 'To Travel This Ship'. Have a go at interpreting this poem — jot down anything you notice about its structure, themes and the techniques the poet uses. Then write an answer for this question: 'How is the experience of emigration presented in the poem?'

Comparing Poems

Comparing poems means looking at the underlined similarities and underlined differences between them. Think about how the poems use all the features covered in this section — form, themes, voice and language techniques.

1. The poem below is 'Farewell' by Anne Brontë.

   The questions below ask you to compare 'Farewell' and 'Ashes of Life' (p. 37).

   > Farewell to thee! but not farewell
   > To all my fondest thoughts of thee:
   > Within my heart they still shall dwell;
   > And they shall cheer and comfort me.
   >
   > O, beautiful, and full of grace!
   > If thou hadst never met mine eye,
   > I had not dreamed a living face
   > Could fancied charms so far outvie*.
   >
   > That voice, the magic of whose tone
   > Can wake an echo in my breast,
   > Creating feelings that, alone,
   > Can make my tranced* spirit blest.
   >
   > That laughing eye, whose sunny beam
   > My memory would not cherish less; —
   > And oh, that smile! whose joyous gleam
   > Nor mortal language can express.
   >
   > Adieu*, but let me cherish, still,
   > The hope with which I cannot part.
   > Contempt may wound, and coldness chill,
   > But still it lingers in my heart.
   >
   > And who can tell but Heaven, at last,
   > May answer all my thousand prayers,
   > And bid the future pay the past
   > With joy for anguish, smiles for tears?

   *outvie — outdo   *Adieu — goodbye   *tranced — entranced

   Reread 'Ashes of Life' on the previous page, then answer the questions below.

   a) The statements below refer to one or both of the poems. Write down the name of the poem each statement refers to. If the statement refers to both poems, write 'both'.

   i) The poem uses first-person narration. ....

   ii) The poem uses religious language. ....

   iii) The narrator is feeling pessimistic. ....

   b) Summarise the narrator's feelings and experiences in each of the poems.

   ....

   ....

   c) i) Write out an example of hyperbole from 'Farewell'.

   ....

   ii) Compare how the poets use figurative language to describe loss.

   d) Look at the form of the poems. Why do you think the poets chose to use these forms?

   e) Compare the tone of the poems. What is the effect of the tone of each poem on the reader?

   f) Write three paragraphs comparing how the poets present loss. Use your answers to the questions above to help you. Make sure you back up each of your points with quotes.

Section 4: Reading — Poetry

Section 5: Reading — Comparing Texts

What's that? You want some practice comparing texts? Well, you've come to the right section. You'll need to use all the skills you've worked on in the previous reading sections, so go back and refresh your memory if you're feeling unsure about anything. When you're ready, give these warm-up questions a try.

Before you Start

1. Read the extracts below, then answer the questions.

   A As I gathered driftwood along the shore, I became aware of a sound I did not recognise — a coarse grunt followed by high-pitched chirps. I had yet to explore beyond my sandy refuge, so my curiosity was piqued...

   After pushing my way through the nearby foliage, I found the source of the eerie noise. A cumbersome creature shuffled towards me, its stumpy wings flapping hysterically as it let out another of its strange calls. I had never seen such a peculiar animal. Its head was large and wide, much like a lion's, with a thick mass of fur obscuring its marble eyes. Its body was almost... reptilian... covered in scales and bony thorns. The longer I stared at it, the more unnerved I became.

   B **RUFFLING SCIENTIFIC FEATHERS**

   Larkdale was abuzz on Monday 5th July when an unidentified feather was found in the forest. Heather Saw found the curious item while out on a walk. "It was staggering to see it just sitting there glistening in the light, its iridescent barbs sparkling. The whole town is enthralled by it and rightly so. I'll be thinking of that beautiful magenta for weeks to come."

   The feather is said to measure nearly a metre long, and has stumped even the country's top scientists. Dr Si Ence described it as "an earth-shattering discovery", adding "It could be indicative of an as-yet-unknown species."

   a) Summarise each text in one sentence.

   ....

   ....

   b) i) Describe the narrator's reaction to their discovery in Text A.
      Use evidence from the text to support your answer.

      ....

      ....

      ....

      ii) How is the reaction to the discovery in Text B different to the reaction in Text A? Support your answer using details from the texts.

   Go back and read the texts again, jotting down some notes as you go.

   c) Compare how language is used to describe the discovery in each extract.

   d) Compare the structure of the extracts. What effect does the structure have on the reader?

Comparing Texts

Now your comparing muscles are nicely warmed up, it's time to compare some bigger texts. I'm giving you not one, not two, but three texts. Read through each one thoroughly and answer the questions that follow.

An extract from an archaeologist's journal called *The Mayan Expedition*

23rd April, 17:23

After clearing the main swathes of vegetation earlier today, we were able to examine the spectacular limestone structures which tower above the tree line. On first inspection, they appear to be in remarkably good condition. Small fragments of rock have been chewed off by the surrounding flora, but astonishingly, a large proportion remains intact. The tallest pyramid is, we believe, a temple, with broad staircases on all sides. Much of the structure is encased in vines. My eagle-eyed colleague spotted some astoundingly intricate carvings obscured by the twisted trunks — our guides are working diligently to free them so that we can study these phenomenal details more closely. There is a central track which slithers through the dense jungle, connecting the pyramids. Straying barely a metre from this rocky serpent plunges you into thick vegetation which even daylight struggles to penetrate. The limestone monoliths along its border are caked in moss, and there are ghostly outlines of other buildings concealed behind the veil of dark green leaves.

24th April, 15:46

I left my colleagues at the site earlier to retrieve further equipment from our base. I must have deviated from the snaking path, as I now find myself lost in this boundless ecosystem, held captive by its leafy embrace. There is nothing to do but write while I await rescue. Sitting here in the searing heat with only the rainforest for company, it is interesting to reflect on the way the Maya were at one with this environment. They understood how to peacefully coexist with its complexities, yet I am reliant on my colleagues to save me. It saddens me to think that human connection with nature is now in such jeopardy.

An extract from a novel called *The Mystery of Camel Manor*

Approaching from the south lawn, the estate agent ushered us towards an immaculately presented building. It stood staunchly before us like a dutiful soldier.

"When I first saw this property it was a ruin — totally entangled in impenetrable thicket. Now, I think you'll agree, it's a magnificent edifice. This main façade was once choked by a sprawling mass of persistent ivy, but that's all been cut back to let the brickwork finally breathe."

She finished her rigmarole, barely stopping to breathe herself. She described the building eloquently, but I couldn't help but feel her speech was *too* eloquent. *Too* rehearsed.

"Observe how the delicate window panes glitter like diamonds in the sun," she began again.

Our eyes followed her gesture. The windows were smooth and unbroken, reflecting a painting of bright blue sky dappled with clouds of fine cotton. Gazing at the flawless vision, I sensed the building had been scrubbed of any character it once had. Standing on the lawn before the house, I could not smell the hyacinths in full bloom, or the musty odour of the bench's damp wood from yesterday's rain. I could smell chemicals, harsh and sterile.

"Surely a traditional house with a garden as grand as this should be protected at all costs? Why did the house fall into disrepair before?" I enquired.

"Everything was in order before the previous owner took up residence. His... delinquency... meant that the house had... minor complications. I assure you it's still brimming with personality..."

Comparing Texts

An extract from *Rebecca* by Daphne du Maurier

Last night I dreamt I went to Manderley again. It seemed to me I stood by the iron gate leading to the drive, and for a while I could not enter, for the way was barred to me. There was a padlock and a chain upon the gate. I called in my dream to the lodge-keeper, and had no answer, and peering closer through the rusted spokes of the gate I saw that the lodge was uninhabited.

No smoke came from the chimney, and the little lattice windows gaped forlorn. Then, like all dreamers, I was possessed of a sudden with supernatural powers and passed like a spirit through the barrier before me. The drive wound away in front of me, twisting and turning as it had always done, but as I advanced I was aware that a change had come upon it; it was narrow and unkept, not the drive that we had known. At first I was puzzled and did not understand, and it was only when I bent my head to avoid the low swinging branch of a tree that I realized what had happened. Nature had come into her own again and, little by little, in her stealthy, insidious way had encroached upon the drive with long, tenacious fingers. The woods, always a menace even in the past, had triumphed in the end. They crowded, dark and uncontrolled, to the borders of the drive. The beeches with white, naked limbs leant close to one another, their branches intermingled in a strange embrace, making a vault above my head like the archway of a church. And there were other trees as well, trees that I did not recognize, squat oaks and tortured elms that straggled cheek by jowl* with the beeches, and had thrust themselves out of the quiet earth, along with monster shrubs and plants, none of which I remembered.

The drive was a ribbon now, a thread of its former self, with gravel surface gone, and choked with grass and moss. The trees had thrown out low branches, making an impediment to progress; the gnarled roots looked like skeleton claws. Scattered here and again amongst this jungle growth I would recognize shrubs that had been landmarks in our time, things of culture and grace, hydrangeas whose blue heads had been famous. No hand had checked their progress, and they had gone native now, rearing to monster height without a bloom, black and ugly as the nameless parasites that grew beside them.

On and on, now east now west, wound the poor thread that once had been our drive. Sometimes I thought it lost, but it appeared again, beneath a fallen tree perhaps, or struggling on the other side of a muddied ditch created by the winter rains. I had not thought the way so long. Surely the miles had multiplied, even as the trees had done, and this path led but to a labyrinth, some choked wilderness, and not to the house at all. I came upon it suddenly; the approach masked by the unnatural growth of a vast shrub that spread in all directions, and I stood, my heart thumping in my breast, the strange prick of tears behind my eyes.

*cheek by jowl — close together

1. Write one sentence that briefly summarises each text.

    The Mayan Expedition: ....

    ....

    The Mystery of Camel Manor: ....

    ....

    Rebecca: ....

    ....

Comparing Texts

2. Complete the table by ticking the boxes next to the statements that apply to each extract.

	The Mayan Expedition	The Mystery of Camel Manor	Rebecca
It uses direct speech.			
The narrator imagines the events in the extract.			
It uses sensory language to describe rock.			
It uses figurative language to describe trees.			

3. Write down the text that best matches each theme.

   nature's destructive power ....

   subduing nature's power ....

   secrets hidden by nature ....

4. How is the purpose of *The Mayan Expedition* different to the purpose of the other extracts?

   ....

5. a) Explain the metaphor that is used to describe the path in *The Mayan Expedition*.

   ....

   ....

   b) In *Rebecca*, the author also uses a metaphor to describe a path. Write out this metaphor.

   ....

   c) Which of these metaphors do you find most effective? Explain your answer.

6. a) Write down one word to describe the estate agent in *The Mystery of Camel Manor*. Explain why you chose this word, using evidence from the text.

   b) Look at the tone of the estate agent's dialogue. Compare her tone to the tone created by the writer of *The Mayan Expedition*.

Section 5: Reading — Comparing Texts © Not to be photocopied

Comparing Texts

7. Give one way that the narrator's experience in *The Mystery of Camel Manor* is different to the narrator's experience in *Rebecca*. Use evidence to explain your answer.

   ....

   ....

   ....

8. a) Write down an example of personification from one of the texts. What is its effect?

   ....

   ....

   ....

   b) Write down an example of personification from another of the texts. Explain its effect.

   ....

   ....

   ....

9. a) 'In *Rebecca* and *The Mayan Expedition*, nature is presented as a powerful and threatening force.' Do you agree with this statement? Explain your answer.

   b) Compare how nature is presented in *The Mystery of Camel Manor* and *Rebecca*. Use evidence from the texts to support your answer.

10. Compare the form and structure of *The Mayan Expedition* and one of the other texts. What effect does the form and structure of these texts have on the reader?

11. Reread *Rebecca* and *The Mayan Expedition*. Compare the setting of each text and the atmosphere it creates. Use evidence from the texts to support your answer.

12. Reread *The Mystery of Camel Manor* and *Rebecca*. Compare the tone of the extracts and examine the effect tone has on the reader.

 Now you've looked at comparing two texts, see whether you can compare all three. Think about how language is used in each text. Try to write at least three paragraphs comparing them, with clearly explained ideas. Use evidence from each of the three texts to back up your points.

Section 6: Reading Review

This is the final reading section, so test your skills with a variety of texts, each with a page of questions. Here's an extract from *Frankenstein* by Mary Shelley. It's narrated by Victor Frankenstein, a scientist.

> It was on a dreary night of November that I beheld the accomplishment of my toils. With an anxiety that almost amounted to agony, I collected the instruments of life around me, that I might infuse a spark of being into the lifeless thing that lay at my feet. It was already one in the morning; the rain pattered dismally against the panes, and my candle was nearly burnt out, when, by the glimmer of the half-extinguished light, I saw the dull yellow eye of the creature open; it breathed hard, and a convulsive* motion agitated its limbs.
>
> How can I describe my emotions at this catastrophe, or how delineate the wretch whom with such infinite pains and care I had endeavoured to form? His limbs were in proportion, and I had selected his features as beautiful. Beautiful! Great God! His yellow skin scarcely covered the work of muscles and arteries beneath; his hair was of a lustrous black, and flowing; his teeth of a pearly whiteness; but these luxuriances only formed a more horrid contrast with his watery eyes, that seemed almost of the same colour as the dun-white sockets in which they were set, his shrivelled complexion and straight black lips.
>
> The different accidents of life are not so changeable as the feelings of human nature. I had worked hard for nearly two years, for the sole purpose of infusing life into an inanimate body. For this I had deprived myself of rest and health. I had desired it with an ardour* that far exceeded moderation; but now that I had finished, the beauty of the dream vanished, and breathless horror and disgust filled my heart. Unable to endure the aspect of the being I had created, I rushed out of the room and continued a long time traversing my bed-chamber, unable to compose my mind to sleep. At length lassitude* succeeded to the tumult* I had before endured, and I threw myself on the bed in my clothes, endeavouring to seek a few moments of forgetfulness. But it was in vain; I slept, indeed, but I was disturbed by the wildest dreams. I thought I saw Elizabeth, in the bloom of health, walking in the streets of Ingolstadt. Delighted and surprised, I embraced her, but as I imprinted the first kiss on her lips, they became livid with the hue of death; her features appeared to change, and I thought that I held the corpse of my dead mother in my arms; a shroud enveloped her form, and I saw the grave-worms crawling in the folds of the flannel. I started from my sleep with horror; a cold dew covered my forehead, my teeth chattered, and every limb became convulsed; when, by the dim and yellow light of the moon, as it forced its way through the window shutters, I beheld the wretch — the miserable monster whom I had created. He held up the curtain of the bed; and his eyes, if eyes they may be called, were fixed on me. His jaws opened, and he muttered some inarticulate sounds, while a grin wrinkled his cheeks. He might have spoken, but I did not hear; one hand was stretched out, seemingly to detain me, but I escaped and rushed downstairs. I took refuge in the courtyard belonging to the house which I inhabited, where I remained during the rest of the night, walking up and down in the greatest agitation, listening attentively, catching and fearing each sound as if it were to announce the approach of the demoniacal corpse to which I had so miserably given life.

*convulsive — jerky
*ardour — great passion
*lassitude — weariness
*tumult — chaos

1. Summarise what happens in this extract.

....

....

....

3 marks

2. a) Write down the part of the extract that tells you the aim of Victor's work.

....

1 mark

b) Explain why the description of the experiment as a "catastrophe" is surprising.

....

....

2 marks

3. a) Describe the atmosphere of the extract.

....

1 mark

b) Using details from the extract, explain how the setting reinforces this atmosphere.

2 marks

4. a) What was Victor's attitude to his work before his experiment succeeded?

....

1 mark

b) How does his attitude change in this extract? Explain why his attitude changes.

2 marks

c) How does Shelley use language to emphasise Victor's feelings in the third paragraph? Use details from the extract to support your answer.

4 marks

5. What do you think is the significance of Victor's nightmare in this extract? Explain your answer using details from the extract.

4 marks

6. Explain how Shelley conveys Victor's view that the creature is monstrous. Support your answer using details from the extract.

6 marks

7. How does Shelley make this extract frightening? Comment on her use of language and structure. Use details from the extract to support your answer.

8 marks

© Not to be photocopied

Section 6: Reading Review

Reading Review

The poem below is *Blessing* by Imtiaz Dharker. Read through the poem carefully, then reread it slowly, looking for different poetic techniques. Finally, have a go at answering the questions on the next page.

> The skin cracks like a pod.
> There never is enough water.
>
> Imagine the drip of it,
> the small splash, echo
> in a tin mug,
> the voice of a kindly god.
>
> Sometimes, the sudden rush
> of fortune. The municipal* pipe bursts,
> silver crashes to the ground
> and the flow has found
> a roar of tongues. From the huts,
> a congregation*: every man woman
> child for streets around
> butts in, with pots,
> brass, copper, aluminium,
> plastic buckets,
> frantic hands,
>
> and naked children
> screaming in the liquid sun,
> their highlights polished to perfection,
> flashing light,
> as the blessing sings
> over their small bones.

*municipal — owned by the local government
*congregation — a group of people gathered for religious worship

Section 6: Reading Review

1. Briefly summarise the event described in the poem.

....

....

☐ 1 mark

2. a) Write down a simile from the poem.

....

☐ 1 mark

b) What does this simile suggest about the poem's setting? Explain your answer.

....

....

☐ 2 marks

3. a) Write down three examples of onomatopoeia from the poem.

....

☐ 1 mark

b) What is the effect of onomatopoeia in the poem? Explain your answer.

☐ 2 marks

4. What does the language used in the third stanza suggest about water?

....

....

☐ 2 marks

5. a) What does "liquid sun" suggest about water?

....

☐ 1 mark

b) Why do you think Dharker chose this description? Explain your answer.

☐ 2 marks

6. Explain how the poem's form reflects the event described in the poem.

☐ 4 marks

7. Describe how the tone changes in the poem. Support your answer with quotes.

☐ 4 marks

8. Explain how Dharker presents water as a religious force in the poem. Support your answer with details from the poem.

☐ 8 marks

© Not to be photocopied

Section 6: Reading Review

Reading Review

The extract below is from *Macbeth* by William Shakespeare. Earlier in the play, Macbeth and Lady Macbeth hatched a plan to kill the king and take his crown. Read through the extract, then answer the questions.

MACBETH: We will proceed no further in this business.
He hath honoured me of late, and I have bought
Golden opinions from all sorts of people,
Which would be worn now in their newest gloss,
Not cast aside so soon.

LADY MACBETH: Was the hope drunk
Wherein you dressed yourself? Hath it slept since?
And wakes it now to look so green and pale
At what it did so freely? From this time,
Such I account* thy love. Art thou afeard
To be the same in thine own act and valour,
As thou art in desire? Wouldst thou have that
Which thou esteem'st the ornament of life*,
And live a coward in thine own esteem,
Letting "I dare not" wait upon "I would",
Like the poor cat i'th'adage*?

MACBETH: Prithee, peace.
I dare do all that may become* a man;
Who dares do more is none.

LADY MACBETH: What beast was't then
That made you break this enterprise* to me?
When you durst* do it, then you were a man.
And to be more than what you were, you would
Be so much more the man. Nor time, nor place
Did then adhere*, and yet you would make both*.
They have made themselves and that their fitness now
Does unmake you. I have given suck and know
How tender 'tis to love the babe that milks me:
I would, while it was smiling in my face,
Have plucked my nipple from his boneless gums
And dashed the brains out, had I so sworn
As you have done to this.

MACBETH: If we should fail?

LADY MACBETH: We fail?
But screw your courage to the sticking-place,
And we'll not fail.

> The "adage" Lady Macbeth refers to here is 'cats like eating fish, but they don't like getting their paws wet'.

*account — estimate the value of
*that / Which thou esteem'st the ornament of life — the crown
*i'th'adage — in the proverb
*may become — is suitable for
*break this enterprise — tell this plan
*durst — dared to
*Did then adhere — were right before
*make both — go ahead

Section 6: Reading Review

1. a) What is Macbeth's attitude to the plan to kill the king at the start of the extract?

....

1 mark

b) In your own words, explain why Macbeth feels this way.

....

....

....

2 marks

2. a) Explain how Lady Macbeth uses personification to persuade Macbeth. Support your answer using examples from the extract.

....

....

....

3 marks

b) Give two other ways Lady Macbeth tries to persuade Macbeth. Use details from the extract to support your answer.

4 marks

3. Aside from being persuasive, describe the tone of Lady Macbeth's dialogue. Use quotes from the extract to support your answer.

4 marks

4. How does Macbeth feel in the lines starting "Prithee, peace."? Explain your answer.

....

....

2 marks

5. Read Lady Macbeth's second speech. What effect does her description of what she would do to the baby have on the reader? Use evidence to explain your answer.

3 marks

6. Give two ways you think the characters should speak and move to emphasise their feelings in the final four lines of the extract. Explain your answer.

4 marks

7. What overall impression of Macbeth do you get from this extract? Explain your answer using details from the extract.

8 marks

© Not to be photocopied

Section 6: Reading Review

Reading Review

The text below is from a magazine article about an indie-rock band's new album. Read through the article a few times, then answer the questions on the next page.

The Simulation — *Dreams of Somewhere*

The Simulation's new album is a fun breath of fresh air (or rather, a roaring tornado) in the traditionally male-dominated indie-rock scene.

On Saturday, during a performance in a pub in Manchester, Sally Ellis (lead singer of indie-rock band The Simulation) told her enraptured crowd, "Big things are coming, big things!", before launching into a whirlwind performance of her new album's first track, 'Living the Dream'. If the crowd's reaction is anything to go by, Ellis might just be right.

When I catch up with Ellis and her bandmates — Chloe Forbes (guitar), Tina Wren (bass) and Mia Cheng (drums) — after the gig, they are still high on adrenaline.

"That was wild," laughs Forbes, squeezing Cheng into a tight hug. The other girls nod enthusiastically, all smiles and jokes. Wren explains that they've been friends since their school days, and it shows: the rebellious energy of missed deadlines, daydreaming and detentions remains palpable in their sound, a hangover from hours of writing lyrics when they should have been doing homework.

"In fact," Cheng butts in, smoothly steering the conversation towards the album, "some of the tracks on *Dreams of Somewhere* reference our school days. I think that those songs are like we're recollecting the past through rose-tinted spectacles which have been cracked and glued back together... they're kind of like a fractured perfection."

Ellis nods, then adds, "Take 'Aspiration Station' — that's about my thirteen-year-old self, "weighed down with potential" (she self-deprecatingly makes air quotes with her fingers) as I desperately tried to please my teachers, parents and friends. The chorus, "Don't forget! Have no regrets!" is all about the contradiction at the heart of being a teenager — you're torn between this intense longing to live in the moment, and an awareness that your academic work now might define your future." Ellis pauses, then grins, "Basically, being a teen *sucks*."

Ellis's comment perfectly sums up the heady mixture of sincerity and playfulness which underpins *Dreams of Somewhere*. The Simulation's second album in as many years, the record picks up where their self-titled debut left off, fusing catchy rhythms with entertaining lyrics which, true to the band's name, depict the world as an illusion. As Wren explains sombrely, life is a "hollow game where everyone's forgotten the rules —"

"So we might as well make up our own!" Forbes chimes in, a cheeky glint in her eye.

This collision of cynical and upbeat is evident throughout their helter-skelter of an album — it's impossible to pin down. The record is somehow playfully profound, angrily euphoric and imperfectly polished. This variety is both a triumph and a curse: to listen from start to finish is to be endlessly surprised and scintillated, yet it is also somewhat like being on a faulty roller coaster which jerks up and down, just about pulls off a loop-the-loop, and leaves you nauseous, a little shaken, but grinning.

When I ask the band about these contradictions, they shrug. "So when you sing, 'Even the bees think the world is a mess', is that meant genuinely?" I probe. Ellis scrunches her forehead into a frown. "We take ourselves *very* seriously," she says. Then she flashes me an unmistakable smirk.

As I re-listen to the album on the way home after the interview, I reach a realisation. Perhaps the band's more profound lyrics don't quite land, but I think that this is the point. The Simulation is itself a simulation: they are *pretending* to be a serious rock group, but it is all a schoolgirl prank, an act of pure rebellion.

At the end of the day, whether you see the band as profound or playful, listening to *Dreams of Somewhere* is *fun*. It's the kind of music that makes you smile, that makes you dance — and that's what good music should do. 'Big things,' indeed.

1. Why is The Simulation different to many other indie-rock bands?

....

1 mark

2. Give two reasons why The Simulation is an appropriate name for the band.

....

....

....

2 marks

3. a) Write out an example of an oxymoron from the review.

An oxymoron is a phrase which combines two contradictory ideas.

....

1 mark

b) What effect do oxymorons have in the text? Explain your answer.

....

....

2 marks

c) Explain how the writer uses figurative language to emphasise their point further.

2 marks

4. Why does the writer end the article with "'Big things,' indeed."? Explain your answer.

....

....

2 marks

5. Give three layout features from the review and explain why the writer uses them.

6 marks

6. How do the band feel about their time at school?
Explain your answer using details from the review.

4 marks

7. Sum up the writer's opinion of *Dreams of Somewhere*. Do you think they would give the album a perfect score? Explain your answer using details from the review.

4 marks

8. How does the writer use language and structure to entertain the reader?
Support your answer using details from the review.

6 marks

© Not to be photocopied

Section 6: Reading Review

Section 7: Writing — Non-Fiction Writing

The time has come to bid farewell to the Reading section and continue on your merry way into the Writing section. This bit is all about getting to grips with non-fiction texts — essays, letters, articles, all that jazz. First, have a go at these warm-up questions to ease yourself into the world of non-fiction.

Before you Start

1. This extract is from a piece of travel writing. Write down an example from the text that supports the point below. Then explain why the example you chose supports the point.

   > Sitting on the waterfront, the water quietly lapping the shore, I watched the sun's slow descent. As it disappeared below the horizon, colours became muted and the air stilled. A drop of my ice cream trickled onto my hand, cold for only a moment on my sun-warmed skin.

   Point: The writer uses sensory descriptions to create a more vivid picture for the reader.

   Example: ....

   Explanation: ....

   ....

2. Write a sentence that would fit the purpose and content of each text below.

   a) A leaflet advising people about what to do if they see a bear in their garden.

   ....

   ....

   b) A newspaper article informing people that a rare species of squid has been discovered.

   ....

   ....

3. The following extract is from a speech. List two persuasive features it uses.

   > The reasons why we should have a town Broccoli Festival are infinite. I mean, what vegetable deserves to be celebrated more than broccoli? It goes with so many different meals, is a healthy side dish and even looks like a miniature tree. We all need to band together to honour this magnificent, marvellous, mouth-watering food.

   ....

   ....

Planning

Although you'll immediately want to get into the thrilling business of non-fiction writing, don't forget to plan first. This will help you work out what you want to write about and stop you from going off-track.

1. Here is a plan for a persuasive letter to the mayor about renaming a local park.

> Introduction: The town will rename a park in honour of local hero, Pamela Peace.
>
> Para 1: She did a lot of cool stuff during her lifetime.
>
> Para 2: Thanks to her, more people were inspired to follow a similar career path. Renaming the park would celebrate the work she did for the community.
>
> Para 3: Some people might be against renaming the park. They are wrong because it would give the town a positive image.
>
> Conclusion: Renaming the park would be great for the town.

a) Rewrite this plan to improve it.

b) Explain why the changes you made in part a) improve the plan.

2. Write a brief plan for one of the tasks below.

| Write a speech arguing that crazy golf should become an Olympic sport. | Write a newspaper article about whether or not people should travel abroad for a holiday. | Write an magazine article about why films are more enjoyable than TV shows. |

Introduction: ....

....

Point 1: ....

....

Point 2: ....

....

Point 3: ....

....

Conclusion: ....

....

3. You've been given this prompt: "Weekends are too short, so they should be extended to three days." Plan a speech which argues for or against this idea. Include an introduction, at least three key arguments and a conclusion.

© Not to be photocopied Section 7: Writing — Non-Fiction Writing

Structure

Doing things in an order that doesn't make any sense? A little bit gross. Oh, I'm talking about brushing your teeth and then drinking orange juice, by the way. Probably should have said that bit first.

1. This is the first draft of a short article for a school magazine.

> **A Passion for Pets**
>
> Here at Windshire School, there are lots of clubs to join. The Friends of Dogs Society is one of them. Keep reading for more details about the society.
>
> Across the UK, thousands of dogs end up in shelters every year. Many of these dogs are given up to the shelters due to their owners being unable to care for them, and some are even abandoned. Although the dogs are cared for at the shelters, their behaviour may be negatively affected by losing their family.
>
> Libby, a Year 12 student, joined the society due to her own experiences with adopting a shelter dog. "When we brought Scout home, he was terrified, always hiding under tables," Libby said. "But now his tail hardly stops wagging!"
>
> If you're like Libby and want to become a Friend of Dogs, join the society today.

a) Rewrite the opening paragraph so that it grabs the reader's attention more effectively.

b) Why do you think the writer put paragraph 3 directly after paragraph 2?

....

....

c) Read the first two paragraphs again. In what way does the second paragraph not follow on effectively from the introduction?

....

....

d) Write a paragraph that could follow on from the introduction. Make sure it keeps the reader interested in the article.

2. The sentences in this paragraph about London have been mixed up. Rewrite the paragraph so that the order of the sentences flows better.

> **One reason for this popularity is that London offers something for everyone: there are countless shops, fascinating museums and an almost endless list of restaurants. In 2019, around 21.7 million people visited London, up 18% from 2015. It is therefore clear that experiencing London is a priority for travellers. Over the years, our capital city has become an increasingly popular tourist destination.**

Section 7: Writing — Non-Fiction Writing

Structure

3. The following extract is from a story about a deep-sea diver.

> Lia sank into the abyss, the gloom intensifying with her descent. Squinting, she struggled to situate herself, the distant glimmers of sunlight offering little assistance. She felt herself shiver, though whether from the low temperature or the thought of what she might discover, she was unsure. With a deep breath and shaking hands, she turned on her torch and swam forward.

a) Imagine you're writing the answer to the following essay:
"'Lia is presented as a brave character.' Do you agree with this statement?"
Write down a point you'd make for this essay, using the information in the story extract.

....

b) Copy a piece of evidence that supports your answer to part a).

....

c) Explain why the evidence you gave in part b) supports your answer to part a).

....

....

....

4. You have been asked to write an essay on this topic:
"'Zombies are better friends to have than werewolves.' Do you agree?"

a) Write down three key points that you would make in your essay.

b) Then write out the conclusion for your essay. Make sure you give a clear answer to the question in the essay title.

5. Your town is hosting its first welly-throwing competition.

a) Plan an article to persuade as many people as possible to get involved in the event.

> i) Write down five points you want to make in your article.
> ii) Choose the three points that you think are the most persuasive.
> iii) Decide on the most logical order for those three points.

b) Using your plan from part a), write the article.

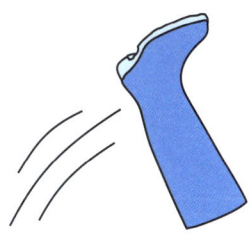

Quoting

Using quotations can hugely improve the quality of your writing. Including specific, relevant evidence from fiction or non-fiction texts that you've studied will help make your analysis focused and convincing.

1. a) These essay extracts include quotations that are too long. Pick out the relevant parts of each quotation and write them on the lines below.

> **A** The description of the party presents it as a negative experience. The narrator says that "Balloons exploded all around me and a blizzard of confetti blinded me." These violent words suggest that the celebration was overwhelming.

> **B** The narrator finds peace when they go to sleep. They write that "When the day is done / And the curtains close, / It is time to feel / A little bit less / In the serenity / Of unconsciousness." This suggests that sleep is a soothing experience for them.

A) ....

B) ....

b) Rewrite each extract so that the shortened version of the quotation fits into it.

2. a) The three example answers below are based on the following extract. For each example answer, explain why the way the writer has used quotations is incorrect.

> Outside, the storm raged on. It roared like a mighty beast, attacking the land with wind as sharp as claws. It howled, hammered and harassed, trying to break through every entrance, infiltrate every home.

> The storm is presented as a powerful force. "It roared like a mighty beast". This simile creates the impression that the storm is strong and aggressive.

i) ....

> Alliteration emphasises the wind's destructive nature. The writer describes how the wind howled, hammered and harassed houses. The repeated 'h' sound suggests that it is relentless.

ii) ....

> The writer uses personification to make the wind seem more threatening. They write that the wind wanted to "intrude" into people's homes. This word implies that the wind has no respect for others.

iii) ....

b) Rewrite each example answer so that it uses the quotation correctly.

Section 7: Writing — Non-Fiction Writing © Not to be photocopied

Writing Essays

Writing an essay might seem like a mammoth task, but when you break it down into chunks, it's not that bad at all. To feel more at ease with essay-writing, have a go at the questions on the next couple of pages.

1. This is an example of an essay plan in response to the prompt: "Write an essay about the potential pros and cons of time travelling."

   > Point 1: Can learn about different time periods, e.g. the Victorian era
   > Point 2: Could experience great historic moments, e.g. the invention of the washing machine
   > Point 3: Might cause family rifts, e.g. dad loves the Stone Age, son prefers the Iron Age
   > Point 4: Could face unusual threats, e.g. dinosaurs, unknown diseases

   a) Write an introduction for this essay, making sure you give a brief overview of your argument.

   b) Write a conclusion for the essay, summing up its key points.

2. Write down three points that you would include in each of the following essays.

   a) "To what extent do you agree that footballers are overpaid?"

   b) "Explain why your favourite film is a masterpiece."

   c) "'All public toilets should be free to use.' Do you agree?"

   d) "How far do you agree that people have become obsessed with the virtual world?"

3. Reread the extract from *Dracula* on p.29, then read this first draft of an essay answer for the question: 'How does the author create an unnerving atmosphere in this extract?'

   > The author uses several techniques to create an unnerving atmosphere in this extract. The use of onomatopoeia in the first paragraph helps the reader to imagine the sounds experienced by the narrator. This allows them to build a clearer picture of what the setting is like. The imagery used to describe the old man evokes the senses to help the reader visualise him — we can imagine the stark contrast of his colourless skin and black clothing 'without a single speck of colour'. His behaviour also adds to the atmosphere. He is initially portrayed as unwelcoming, but then becomes more enthusiastic after the narrator has entered his home, and this creates an unnerving atmosphere.

   a) Split the answer into an introduction and three main paragraphs, using '//' to show where each new paragraph should begin.

   b) How would you improve each paragraph in the essay?

   c) Write a conclusion for this essay, making sure to summarise its main points.

© Not to be photocopied   Section 7: Writing — Non-Fiction Writing

Writing Essays

4. Below is a plan for an essay.

> Introduction: Hot and cold weather both have advantages and disadvantages.
>
> Paragraph 1: Hot weather advantages — ice cream and barbecues; don't have to wear bulky clothing
>
> Paragraph 2: Hot weather disadvantages — heat keeps people inside; can get sweaty and sunburned
>
> Paragraph 3: Cold weather advantages — warm clothes can make you feel cosy; if it snows you can make a snowman/have a snowball fight
>
> Paragraph 4: Cold weather disadvantages — can't stay outside for too long without getting cold; ice can make travelling dangerous
>
> Conclusion: Pros and cons of both; I prefer hot weather

a) Write down an essay question that matches this plan.

   ....

b) Write this essay out in full, including the above points as well as one advantage and one disadvantage of hot or cold weather of your own.

5. Here is an essay prompt: "Argue that museums should be more exciting places to visit."

   a) Write the opening sentence of the introduction for the essay.

   ....

   b) Jot down four main points to cover, then choose the strongest three to use in your essay.

   ....

   ....

   ....

   ....

   c) Write the closing statement of the essay.

   ....

   ....

   d) Write the full essay, using your answers to the questions above to help you.

You're not done with essays just yet — there's still room for a bit more practice. I'm feeling nostalgic, so have a look back at the prompts in Q2 on p.57. Choose one to write an essay on, using the points you came up with to help you. Don't forget to use formal language, keep your answer relevant to the question and explain all of your points as clearly as you can.

Section 7: Writing — Non-Fiction Writing © Not to be photocopied

Formal and Informal Language

Greetings. A most warm welcome to this page about formal and informal writing. I sincerely hope you find these questions of use in your endeavour to improve your writing. In other words — hey there, on you go.

1. a) Write whether each of these sentences uses formal or informal language.

   i) She was astounded by Arthur's horrific manners. ....

   ii) I legged it away from the dodgy-looking horse. ....

   iii) Santiago was chuffed about getting some top-quality grub. ....

   iv) Jo requested that Malachi join her for a conversation. ....

   b) Rewrite the formal sentences using informal language, and the informal sentences using formal language.

2. The following extract is from a speech to a school assembly.

> Thanks for gathering here today. I'm going to discuss the important matter of installing vending machines in our school. These machines are vital to the happiness of students and teachers alike, as they provide us with various delicacies and pick-me-ups throughout the day. Some folks would argue that the treats commonly found in vending machines are junk, but I propose that healthy alternatives be provided alongside the usual suspects like chocolate bars and sweets. This would encourage thought about having a more balanced lifestyle.

   a) Underline the parts of the speech which don't fit with its formal style.

   b) Rewrite the speech, correcting the parts you have underlined so they use formal language.

3. The following letter is written using informal language. Rewrite this letter using formal language.

> Hey Mr Anderson,
>
> It'd be awesome if you'd hire me as a receptionist at your law firm. I have a real knack for organising stuff, and I'd always give you my all. I've got bucketloads of work experience, like the summer I worked in a restaurant and the volunteering gig I've got at my local library. They're not jobs in law, but hopefully they'll give me an edge over the other candidates.
>
> Thanks a bunch!
>
> Julius Weber

 So how would you describe yourself? Are you one of the formal folk or an informal individual? Choose one of these writing styles and write an article about the opening of a new attraction in your town. Think about who your audience is and what sort of attraction they'd be interested in.

Writing to Inform, Explain and Advise

Way back when (in Section 1), you dabbled with the different purposes of texts. The next four pages will give you a more in-depth look into some of those purposes, so grab your eggs and let's get cracking...

1. This is an extract from an email about an upcoming hiking trip.

> Weather permitting, we will leave at 9 am sharp on Monday the 13th November. The hike will last for approximately seven hours, which includes a half-hour break for lunch. As the route is not particularly strenuous, minimal equipment is needed. The guides do recommend, however, that everybody brings enough food and water to last longer than the anticipated duration of the hike, in case of unexpected changes to the schedule.

a) What is the main purpose of this text? Circle one option.

to explain   to entertain   to inform   to persuade

b) Choose two features of the text and explain how they support your answer to part a).

....

....

2. A student made a list of points about why their summer holiday was the best one yet. Imagine you're the student who wrote the list. Write the text out in full, making sure to include explanations of why these points made your holiday fun.

> - Played sports all day
> - Visited places that I had never been to before
> - Learned how to cook new recipes
> - Redecorated my childhood bedroom

3. The following extract is from a text that advises students how to do well in interviews.

> You could also consider talking about your hobbies. Clubs and hobbies can be useful when it comes to interviews for jobs or courses — they're a great way to demonstrate your interest in a topic or your skills in a certain area. They also help to show the interviewer that you're a well-rounded, outgoing person. Before the interview, you should write notes about why your hobby is relevant to the job or course. This will help you to get off to a great start in talking about your experiences.

a) Write down another piece of advice the author could have included in their text.

b) Pick a hobby or club. Write a newsletter article giving advice to students looking to join this club.

Section 7: Writing — Non-Fiction Writing

Writing to Inform, Explain and Advise

4. Use the information below to write a blog post explaining the importance of exercise.

- Exercise releases endorphins that improve your mood.
- Exercise can reduce the risk of illness.
- Approximately 1.4 billion adults do not exercise enough.
- 27% of diabetes cases are caused by being inactive.
- Exercise improves your sleep.
- Adults should do 150 minutes of exercise each week.

5. The following text is from a gardening magazine.

> **If you want to attract more pollinators to your garden, make sure you've got plenty of plants that flower year-round. Having a near-constant supply of garden blooms will benefit all insect visitors. Plants with flat, open flowers are much easier for some insects to land on, so try to provide a selection of these among your flowerbeds. Instead of keeping your lawn short throughout the year, give it a chance to grow tall and wild. Common lawn plants like daisies are a particular favourite of hoverflies, whose larvae feed on garden pests like aphids.**

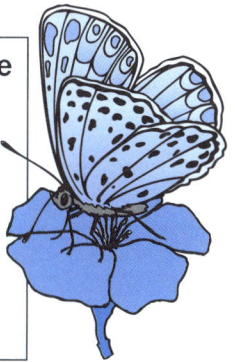

a) What is the main purpose of this text?

....

b) Explain why this text is effective at achieving its purpose.

....

....

....

c) You've been asked to write an article for a magazine on one of the topics below. Choose one, then write down the text's purpose and the main features of that text type.

- how to protect yourself from vampires
- how to choose the right pet dragon
- how to win the trust of a unicorn
- how to avoid getting lost in an enchanted forest

 Imagine you've met someone who doesn't know what a smartphone is. Write a short text informing them what a smartphone is, explaining the benefits of owning one and giving them advice on how to use one. Try to include at least six different points in your text.

Writing to Persuade and Argue

It's time to tackle the delicate arts of persuading and arguing. If you're looking for more effective ways to convince people to agree with you or to get your point across, then this is the topic for you...

1. **Rewrite the following sentences to make them more persuasive.**

   a) The hotel is a popular choice for families because it has plenty of good-quality facilities.

   ....

   ....

   b) Anyone who likes outdoor sports would enjoy visiting the woodland activity centre.

   ....

   ....

   c) You could settle for a boring cheddar, or you could choose a delicious brie.

   ....

   ....

2. **Here are some arguments about why a nearby village should install a speed camera. Use them to write a persuasive speech on the topic.**

   | If drivers won't respond to speed limit signs, the council must install a speed camera. | I strongly recommend that the council take action before the unspeakable happens. | Why sit around and wait for an accident to happen? |

   | If this speeding isn't dangerous enough, the busy road runs right next to a children's play park. | Let's save the spirit of our tranquil village. | If you care about our village, you'll join us in our fight for more traffic-calming measures to keep our community safe. |

   | Make a quick plan to work out the best order for the points and how you're going to use different persuasive language devices. | Cameras are reliable, effective, and a major deterrent. | Speed cameras are miles cheaper to install than bumps and bollards. |

Section 7: Writing — Non-Fiction Writing

Writing to Persuade and Argue

3. The following text argues that ham and pineapple is the best pizza topping.

> Despite being an unusual flavour combination, ham and pineapple is much more exciting than other standard pizza toppings like pepperoni. It provides the perfect balance between sweet and savoury flavours. The refreshing pineapple chunks complement the saltiness of the ham and make it instantly more enjoyable.

a) Write down three arguments for why ham and pineapple is a bad pizza topping.

b) Use these points to write a short text arguing that ham and pineapple is the worst pizza topping.

4. a) Which of these texts is more convincing? Explain your answer.

> **A** All schools should introduce afternoon naps to their timetables. Many students feel stressed on a daily basis and would benefit from having more time to relax. The current breaks in the day are not sufficient to allow students to recharge between lessons. Afternoon naps will help to improve students' concentration and make them more attentive in lessons.

> **B** It could be said that video games offer players a more immersive experience than board games. Virtual reality allows players to become part of an artificial world and feel more connected to what they're playing. It's difficult to replicate this with a standard board game. It's often the case that video games also have more exciting plots and a wider range of characters.

b) Rewrite the text that is less convincing to make it more persuasive.

5. Write a speech arguing **either** in favour of banning mobile phones in schools **or** against it. Your text must mention all the points in the box below.

- Mobile phones are a distraction during lessons.
- Students with expensive mobile phones are a target for thieves.
- Students who don't have a mobile phone are a target for bullies.
- Students need a mobile phone in school so they can keep in touch with their families.
- Mobile phones can be used to take photos of homework tasks or class notes.
- Mobile phones can be used during lessons to aid learning, e.g. through virtual reality.

Section 8: Writing — Fiction Writing

A small word of advice: you'll never win an argument with fictional characters — their minds are completely made up... Anyway, you've read plenty of fiction in the reading section, so I think you're qualified to write some cracking works yourself. Psst, don't worry — we'll still give you heaps of handy tips along the way.

Before you Start

1. Below are some pictures of different characters.

   A   B   C   D

   a) Match each character to the description of a setting below by writing A-D in the boxes.

   | The silence in the hall attested to the fact that the crowd had been enchanted by the speaker's wisdom. | ☐ | The corridors, full of exhausted employees, were a labyrinth of harsh lighting and tired carpets. | ☐ |

   | A veil of red velvet curtains drew back to reveal ornate cardboard scenery and old-fashioned furniture. | ☐ | Beady eyes turned expectantly to the stage as the chime of champagne flutes hushed. | ☐ |

   b) Choose one of the characters above, then write a description of their personality. Make sure you use their actions to help describe them.

   ....

   ....

   ....

2. Write a suitable opening and closing sentence for the story idea below.

   An elderly fisherman comes across a message in a bottle directing him to a great fortune.

   Opening: ....

   ....

   Closing: ....

   ....

Section 8: Writing — Fiction Writing © Not to be photocopied

Planning

I know, you've heard it all before — fail to plan and plan to fail. I won't drone on about the necessity of a plan to make your writing shine, but trust me on this one. I didn't plan my birthday party — nobody came.

1. Have a look at the plan below.

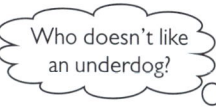

   1. Introduce the main character, Charlie. (A town has elected its first ever mayor — a dog called Charlie.)
   2. Charlie walks through the town being stroked by all of his supporters.
   3. Explain that the setting is a suburban town. A minority of humans (cat lovers, mostly) seek to overthrow Charlie's rule.
   4. Describe what Charlie is like. Maybe Charlie could defeat the resistance in a stand-off or use techniques to fend them off, like puppy dog eyes, etc. Or there could be a plot twist where one of Charlie's friends can actually shapeshift to become a human to reason with them?
   5. Introduce another problem for Charlie to fix. (Ending: everyone lives happily ever after.)

   a) Why is it ineffective to use "etc." in a story plan?

   ....

   b) How do you think this plan could be improved? Give two suggestions.

   ....

   ....

   c) Rewrite the plan so that it includes the changes you recommended in part b).

2. Read through this plan for a short science fiction story.

   - A food critic walks into a popular restaurant. She asks for the 'special' and is given a plate of spaghetti and meatballs. She takes a bite and spits it back out.
   - She asks to see the chef. The waiter looks uneasy. An alien appears from the kitchen.
   - She threatens to write an exposé of the restaurant, so the aliens abduct her out of fear. They take her back to their planet, which is made completely of spaghetti.
   - She tries the local cuisine and writes a glowing review. They take her home.

   a) Why is this an effective plan?

   b) Rewrite the last three bullet points of the plan so that it is appropriate for each of the story genres below. You can add more bullet points wherever necessary.

   i) horror   ii) mystery   iii) comedy

 You should now have three perfectly written plans from Q2, all just waiting for their moment in the spotlight. Well, I think it's time to give one of them their big break. Choose one of the genres above and write out your story in full, using the points in your plan to assist you.

Structure

My favourite structure? Well, I quite like a skyscraper, but you can't deny the value of a good bridge. Oh, you mean story structures... sorry. Just like buildings, your stories need a good structure or they will collapse.

1. Fill in the gaps in this passage about different plot structures.

   | cliffhanger   perspectives   flashforward   narrative   flashback |

   When a story jumps back in time, this is called a .... When it jumps ahead in time, this is called a .... Sometimes, authors will use a .... to help keep readers totally gripped by the story. A split .... is a story told from two different ....

2. The plot points in this story have been jumbled up.

   - Armed with her rolling pin, Grandma follows them, shouting for them to stop.
   - Written on the wall in tomato sauce is "It's my turn to get a slice of the pie. Your pizzeria will never make any dough again, as long as I live."
   - The figure responds to Grandma's shouts by throwing pepperoni at her.
   - Grandma's famous pizza recipe is stolen from the locked safe.
   - Across the road, she sees a hooded figure with a tomato-stained piece of paper.

   This guy is a pizza work...

   a) Put the plot points in the correct order.

   b) Write two plot points to follow directly after this.

   ....

   ....

   c) Which do you think is the best opening sentence? Explain why it is the most effective.

   A) Grandma saved the pizzeria yesterday. This is how she did it.

   B) The pizzeria is in danger and only Grandma can save it.

   C) How many people on earth can say they've literally caught someone red-handed?

   d) How could you use the text's structure to add a sense of suspense to the story?

   ....

   ....

   e) How would you end the story? Explain why your idea would make an effective ending.

   NOW TRY THIS — Now you've jotted down a few ideas to upgrade this story, have a go at writing it out in full. Use your answers above to help you, and make sure you include structural techniques to keep the reader interested — don't forget about all the interesting plot structures you covered in Q1.

Section 8: Writing — Fiction Writing

Building Character

Characters are unapologetically themselves — everything they say and do is a reflection of their personality. They're the stars of the show and boy, do I envy them for that... but I suppose this is all character building.

1. a) Write down an adjective to describe each character below.

    i) She came alive around others, her eyes a little brighter, her smile a little wider.

    ii) He didn't look like much, but he was alert to everything. Any movement, any sound.

    iii) She knew the power of her own voice, and she wouldn't be talked over.

   b) Explain why you chose each adjective.

   ....

   ....

   ....

2. Three different characters said each of the following statements. Write a character description of each one, referring to their actions, words and what they might be thinking. You could also include details about their appearance.

   | "Leave him behind. He's slowing us down anyway." | "I have a full itinerary for tomorrow. Nobody is going to be late, okay?" | "I have to go back inside! People are still trapped in there!" |

3. Read through the character descriptions below. Rewrite them so that their character traits are not explicitly named, but implied through what the characters say and do.

   > Charlotte was painfully shy and rarely seen at social events. A rather unfortunate peculiarity of hers was that she had an extreme fear of sunlight, which wasn't helped by her pale skin's inclination to burn.

   > Jude was always organised and he could be depended upon to have everything worked out. He was efficient and methodical but very, very stubborn. He had a burning hatred for being wrong, along with an intense dislike of pets.

   > Amal was fiercely competitive — some may even say she was ruthless. She was fiery, which was a useful quality to have. The only real thing that held her back in life was how gullible she was. Oh, and her love of sleeping.

Now Try This — It's time to think about how characters interact — what they think of each other and how they might address one another. Write down a conversation between two of the characters from Q2. Remember to think about their personalities and how that might influence the way they speak.

Building Setting

Setting is all about when and where your fiction text takes place — it helps you convey a certain mood to the reader. The beauty of fiction is that it could happen anywhere at all, so let your imagination run wild.

1. Read this description of a setting.

   > The path stretched out in front of us like bait leading prey to peril. The sun mocked us with the occasional slash of light, but each time it retreated back behind the lifeless clouds. Light was dwindling. The trees seemed to jostle us forward, impelling us at least another mile down the path, where we discovered a menacing, grey tower. It seemed to grow taller and taller with every step forward, glowering at us like a king holding court.

   a) What kind of atmosphere does this setting create? Explain your answer.

   ....

   ....

   b) Which genre could this setting be used in? Explain why.

   c) Rewrite the paragraph twice so that the setting would be appropriate for a fairytale and a mystery text. Make sure you create a suitable atmosphere for each genre.

2. Read this description of a character.

   > He reached into the pockets of his jeans that were stained with last night's meal, embellished with this morning's toothpaste. Empty. He had lost his wallet again.

   a) i) Imagine you are introducing this character. What setting would you create for him?

   ....

   ....

   ii) What atmosphere would this setting create? Explain why it would be effective.

   ....

   ....

   b) Write a paragraph that describes this setting in detail.

3. Write a paragraph describing a setting that would be suitable for each of the story titles below. Make sure you create a different atmosphere for each title.

   i) Where the River Flows   ii) Breathing on Mars   iii) A Midsummer Love

 Flick back to page 24 and read over the extract again. Continue the description of the setting by writing your own paragraph describing what the inside of Baskerville Hall might be like. Try to match the author's style of writing, and the atmosphere he has already created in the extract.

Section 8: Writing — Fiction Writing © Not to be photocopied

Writing Stories

They say we've all got a book in us, so you should breeze through this story-writing thing. Funnily enough, I actually did write a best-selling novel once. I won't bore you with the details — it's kind of a long story...

1. a) Write an opening sentence for a story in each of the genres below.

> adventure   science fiction   historical fiction

b) Explain why each of your opening sentences is effective.

2. Imagine you're going to write a short story about being trapped in severe weather conditions.

a) Which point of view would you use? Why?

....

....

b) i) Write down two words that describe the mood you would create in your story.

....

ii) Write down some figurative language that you could use to help create this mood.

....

....

c) What setting would you use to create an appropriate atmosphere?

....

....

3. Choose one of the plot ideas below, then answer the questions.

> **A** Francesca wakes up in an unfamiliar house. She goes downstairs, where she is greeted by two unknown adults who call her by a different name.

> **B** A scientist discovers a secret portal to a parallel universe. When she travels there, she is alarmed when she meets another version of herself.

a) Write a plan for your chosen plot idea. Remember to think about characters, structure, point of view, and the atmosphere you want to create.

b) Using your plan, write the story.

© Not to be photocopied   Section 8: Writing — Fiction Writing

Writing Scripts

Ahh... what's my line again? Oh yes, scripts. When writing a script, you need to give your actors some handy hints with stage directions suggesting how they could perform the dialogue. And... action.

1. Write down some stage directions to describe how an actor could perform these lines.

"It was all his idea." ....

"I'm not feeling quite right." ....

"Please trust me on this." ....

"This doesn't feel safe." ....

"You'd better take a seat." ....

2. Have a look at this extract from a story.

> I stormed up the drive, unable to quell my temper. Approaching my rival, I clenched my fists, ready to challenge him on his crime.
>
> "You stole my bike!" I yelled.
>
> He rolled his eyes. "What would I want with that?" he replied.
>
> "I saw you! You're nothing more than a pathetic thief! Give it back!" My breathing quickened as I grew more and more infuriated, anger bubbling inside of me.

Ahh... I probably deserved that...

a) Adapt the extract into a script. Come up with names for the characters and make sure you use suitable stage directions.

b) Write a stage direction to introduce this scene's setting at the beginning of the script.

....

....

c) Write the next few lines of the script.

3. Read the summary below.

> **A scientist has just discovered the cure for the common cold. Afraid of going bust as a result of this, the CEO of a tissue company kidnaps him to stop the public finding out.**

a) Write a scene based on this summary. Think about how the characters would feel, and how you could express this through dialogue and stage directions.

b) Write the script for the entire short play, making sure to include stage directions.

 You can turn any story into a script if you use dialogue and stage directions. Flick back to the short story you wrote on page 69. Adapt the story into a script, introducing the setting with stage directions. Add in any additional dialogue you think is necessary for the script to make sense.

Section 8: Writing — Fiction Writing © Not to be photocopied

Poetry

You've read plenty of poems across this book so far, so I'm hereby granting you your poetic licence — it's a bit like a driving licence, except completely different. Anyhow, it's time to channel your inner poet...

1. The poem below is about night-time.

    > Stars sparkle brightly like nature's lanterns,
    > Wisdom twinkles in the eyes of barn owls,
    > Fireflies perform a gleeful dusk moondance,
    > Silence breathes gently as life presses pause.

    a) How many syllables are in each line?

    ....

    b) i) Write down three adjectives to describe the poem's mood.

    ii) What mood would you try to create in a poem about daytime?

    c) Write down some figurative language that you could use to describe daytime.

    d) Using the poem above as a template, write a poem about daytime.

2. The poem below is about reading.

    > My bookshelf holds a million lives,
    > I'm Farmers, Athletes, Vets, Midwives,
    >
    > An astronaut, a king, a queen,
    > I'm every character and scene,
    >
    > Now who will I become today —
    > A spy, a dog, a runaway?
    >
    > My characters are limitless,

    a) Add another line to finish the last stanza.

    b) Add three more stanzas to finish the poem.

    Make sure you mimic the rhyme scheme used in the poem so far. Don't forget to use 8 syllables in each line too.

3. Write a poem based on one of the topics below. Include everything in the checklist.

    - a person's shadow
    - sitting on a busy train
    - snorkelling in a coral reef
    - a time capsule's contents

    ☐ The poem has a regular rhyme scheme.
    ☐ Each line in the poem is 7 syllables long.
    ☐ The tone of the poem is appropriate for the topic.
    ☐ Figurative language has been used.

Section 8: Writing — Fiction Writing

Section 9: Writing — Writing Properly

When you're writing, coming up with great ideas is only part of the process. You also need to check your work to make sure that you've used paragraphs properly, your punctuation is tip-top and there are no spelling mistakes. Have a go at the questions on the next few pages to practise checking for these things.

Before you Start

1. Tick the words and phrases that can be used to link paragraphs.

a) Additionally ☐ d) Therefore ☐

b) It was discovered that ☐ e) On the other hand ☐

c) In spite of this ☐ f) It is suggested ☐

2. Circle the words below that are spelt wrong. Rewrite them so they are spelt correctly.

    comparitive   acknowledge   accomodate

    experience   neccessery   occasion

3. Briefly explain how punctuation is used incorrectly in each sentence below. Rewrite each sentence, correcting the mistakes you've identified.

a) I will need several items to reach that ball; a rope, a ladder and a big stick.

....

....

b) "Somebody devoured all the cupcakes!" He roared. "they were on the counter!"

....

....

c) It is a well known fact that camping holidays are superior to all others.

....

....

Structuring Your Writing

Using paragraphs properly and varying your sentence lengths are really important skills when it comes to communicating your ideas. I've found that shouting at a piece of paper is nowhere near as effective...

1. Explain how different sentences are used to affect the pace of these extracts.

   A) Icy air nipped at Timo's face. He was hurtling down the slope. Speed rising, he gripped his poles a little tighter. Dots of faces vanished before he had even computed that they were there. Timo was flying.

   B) With the utmost care and respect for the fabric, Patsy shadowed the material's faint pencilled-in pattern with her needle and thread, swooping in and out to fashion a line of perfectly formed stitches.

2. The extract below is from an adventure story. Rewrite the extract so it uses paragraphs correctly. Number each of your changes, then write down a reason for each one.

   > Anjeli turned the corner of the maze to find another dead end. "We'll never get out," she groaned. But her brother Farhan was undeterred. "Don't say that," he said, turning back around. "We'll just try again." Anjeli resignedly trudged after him. Only an hour ago, she had been standing atop a hill looking down at the maze, thinking that navigating it would be easy.
   > But amidst the towering hedges, her confidence dwindled. Finally, they reached another corner. Anjeli's eyes were unexpectedly blinded by sunlight pouring through a wide gap.

3. The text below is a speech about robots.

   > This speech will argue the benefits of robots.
   >   Many people are nervous about intelligent robots. Though more intelligence usually means robots can carry out tasks more effectively, there are some concerns that it could lead to them taking over the world. The notion is disturbing but there is absolutely no evidence this will happen.
   >   Robots can be helpful for people with limited mobility or dexterity. Having a robot to perform small duties like vacuuming can make a massive difference to the quality of life of those who find it challenging to perform these tasks.
   >   In conclusion, it's clear that having robots in our lives will be massively beneficial. The ability to programme their tasks means that results will be more precise and of a better standard.

   a) Rewrite the introduction so that it makes the argument of the speech clearer.

   ....

   ....

   b) Suggest two ways you could change the two middle paragraphs to make the argument flow better. Explain how the changes would do this.

   c) i) Explain how the conclusion to this speech could be improved.

      ii) Rewrite the conclusion to the speech, correcting the problems you identified in part i).

© Not to be photocopied   Section 9: Writing — Writing Properly

Redrafting and Proofreading

When you finish a piece of writing, check it for anything that needs a rethink. Chances are you'll spot some spelling or punctuation mistakes, or realise that you could word something much better than you did before.

1. The following extract is from the first draft of a short story.

   > Alice ignored the phone that was ringing loudly downstairs, but it kept on ringing and it seemed to be getting louder so finally she got up from her bed and answered it.
   > "Hello?" she said. No response. "Hello?" she said again. It was quiet on the other end of the line. She went to hang up. Then she heard a voice.
   > "Alice," the voice whispered, "listen carefully." Alice recognised the voice. It was her sister. "Don't ask any questions," her sister said. "Just go to my room, grab my bag and meet me in the woods." So Alice grabbed the bag and went to the woods.

   a) Rewrite the first sentence so that it is easier to understand.   *You might want to split the sentence up into shorter ones.*

   ....

   ....

   ....

   b) The last sentence isn't very exciting. Redraft it so that it is more engaging for the reader.

   ....

   ....

   ....

   c) Now redraft the rest of the extract, rewriting anything that you think needs to be improved.

2. The text below contains some spelling and punctuation mistakes.

   a) Proofread the text, underlining all the mistakes.

   > Radio stations are being encureged to stop playing 'Dance-aster'; a song that entered the charts last tuesday. The tune, predicted to be a global sensation, is now a global frustration, some who hear it find themselves unable to stop dancing. Earlier this afternoon: a local supermarket had to close after a group of shopper's effected by the tune trampled the entire fruit and vegatable section to a pulp. "It was unbelieveably bizarre." remarked one witness, who wishes to remain anonimous.
   > If youre wondering how to deal with people overpowered by the need to groove, they're are some things you can do; keep your distance, try to turn the song of, or dance along with them!

   b) Rewrite the text, correcting all of the mistakes.

Section 9: Writing — Writing Properly

Section 10: Writing — Making It Interesting

I think I speak for everyone when I say some texts can be a real drag to read... So don't settle for the same simple vocabulary or short, uninteresting sentences in your own writing. Add some spice with different words and more varied sentences — your writing will be so much better for it.

Before you Start

1. Replace each word with a more interesting word with a similar meaning.

   a) very .... d) angry ....

   b) begin .... e) big ....

   c) allow .... f) said ....

2. Complete the passage by replacing the words in brackets with more interesting synonyms.

   The shire horse .... (walked) steadily down the dusty farm track,

   .... (pulling) a cart laden with produce destined for the local market.

   A .... (cool) breeze .... (blew) through the fields of wheat.

   High in the sky, the sun .... (shone) brightly, casting golden shadows across

   the landscape. The .... (tired) farmer yawned and drove the horse on.

3. a) The following extracts are poorly written. Suggest how each of them could be improved.

   i) It was half past midnight when I woke up. It was blowing a gale outside, which caused the windows to rattle violently. It was ice-cold inside my bedroom.

   ....

   ii) Nobody had expected it to be such a spectacular show because the actors weren't very well known and the director had never worked on such a huge production before.

   ....

   iii) The wallpaper they'd chosen was unbelievably ugly. It had ugly swirling patterns in ugly colours which made the living room look ugly.

   ....

   b) Rewrite each extract, making the improvement you suggested in part a).

Using Different Techniques

Using a variety of sentence lengths and interesting comparisons are great ways to improve the quality of your writing. You should also avoid using too many clichés — these can make your work sound less original.

1. Write out a replacement for the underlined clichés, using more interesting language.

   A cliché is a figure of speech that's used so often that it's lost its impact.

   a) Anyone who attempted the stunt needed <u>nerves of steel</u>.

   ....

   b) The children <u>lost track of time</u> while they were playing.

   ....

   c) I was <u>scared out of my wits</u> after touring the haunted house.

   ....

   d) "No problem," said the mechanic. "I'll have this fixed <u>in a flash</u>."

   ....

2. Complete the sentences below with a suitable comparison. Try to use interesting descriptions.

   a) The diamond shone ....

   b) Mike's scooter is ....

   c) My parrot sings ....

   d) The gloves are ....

   e) Her hair was ....

3. Rewrite the passage, removing any repetition and altering the sentence lengths to make it read better.

   > Sarah was sitting in a chair on the lawn. She listened fondly to the birdsong. It was echoing from the nearby trees. Sarah fondly watched a blackbird hop agilely across the lawn. The blackbird paused, looking for the tell-tale wriggle of worms among the blades of grass, then the blackbird dropped its head in a blur, and came up with a wriggling worm which was protesting its fate.

Do you mind?!

Section 10: Writing — Making It Interesting

Figurative Language

If you really want your writing to stand out, you can use more complex language techniques like hyperbole and extended metaphors. They'll add an extra splash of pizzazz and impress the socks off the reader.

1. Rewrite each sentence below so that it uses hyperbole.

> Hyperbole is when a writer uses exaggeration for effect.

   a) We waited to get into the aquarium.

   ....

   b) The suitcase was heavy.

   ....

2. Write a sentence to describe each object below, using the figurative language technique given in brackets. Each sentence should appeal to a different sense.

   a) disco ball (a metaphor)

   ....

   b) wind chime (onomatopoeia)

   ....

   c) ice cream (alliteration)

   ....

3. Continue the descriptions to turn each metaphor into an extended metaphor.

   a) The crowded train carriage was an oven.

   b) The trees were soldiers standing in a line.

> An extended metaphor is a metaphor which is developed in detail over several sentences.

4. Rewrite the passage below so it uses at least three of the figurative language techniques from this page.

> Dust rose from the desert sand. The horizon blurred and rippled with every step I took. The breeze had disappeared, and I felt the sun on my neck. To the north, I could see rolling sand dunes. They could offer shade, I thought, which was more than could be said for where I currently was.

 Look back at the text you rewrote in Q3 on p.76. See if you can continue the text using the techniques you've covered on the last few pages. Try to include hyperbole, extended metaphors and interesting comparisons.

© Not to be photocopied   Section 10: Writing — Making It Interesting

Section 11: Writing Review

Now that you're an accomplished writer, it's time to put the skills you learnt in this half of the book into practice for one last hurrah. The questions on this page will guide you through writing a script.

> Your drama teacher has asked you to write a short script for this year's school production.
> I want you to write a script for a play about a bank heist. The robbery should be carried out by two criminals, and it should involve interesting action and dialogue. Make sure you include some helpful stage directions for the actors, and don't forget to end the play with a satisfying resolution.

1. a) What atmosphere would you want the setting to create?

   ....

   1 mark

   b) Write down a stage direction that would help you create this atmosphere.

   1 mark

2. a) Write down three adjectives to describe the character traits of each criminal.

   ....

   ....

   2 marks

   b) Choose one of the adjectives you wrote down for each character in part a). Describe how the characters' actions and dialogue will reflect this adjective.

   2 marks

   c) Briefly summarise the relationship between the two criminals.

   2 marks

   d) Write down a stage direction that reflects this relationship.

   1 mark

3. a) Write down the criminals' motive for the bank heist.

   ....

   1 mark

   b) Explain how this motive affects the criminals' actions.

   1 mark

4. Using your answers above, plan your script. Make sure it has an engaging opening, at least three plot developments and a satisfying ending.

   5 marks

5. Now write your script in full. Make sure you check through your writing at the end for any mistakes.

   10 marks

Section 11: Writing Review © Not to be photocopied

Writing Review

Great, now it's time to put your non-fiction knowledge under the microscope for the final time. Gosh, I feel a bit emotional... The questions on this page will help you write a newspaper article.

> Your local newspaper is running a piece on the rise in graffiti in your town. The newspaper wants to hear the opinion of a young person.
>
> We would like you to write an opinion piece about the recent rise in graffiti in our town. We want to know whether you think graffiti should be viewed as vandalism and therefore punished, or if it should be considered a form of art. Make sure you consider both sides of the argument, and give reasons to support your point of view.

An opinion piece is an article that gives the author's opinion about a subject.

1. a) What do you think the tone of your article should be? Explain why.

....

....

2 marks

b) What do you need to do in your article to create this tone?

....

....

2 marks

2. a) Firstly, decide which side of the issue you are going to come down on. Briefly plan three arguments to support your opinion, plus an introduction and conclusion.

5 marks

b) Plan each of the points you will argue in more detail. Make sure you include evidence or examples to back up each point.

6 marks

3. a) Write down a reason why someone might not agree with your opinion.

....

1 mark

b) Write a response to this reason, explaining why it is wrong. Make sure you include evidence to support your response.

2 marks

4. Using your answers to the questions above, write the full article. Make sure you write at least one paragraph for each point, and include the counter-argument and your response from question 3.

10 marks

When you've finished writing your article, make sure you read through it to check for any mistakes.

Writing Review

You're officially on the home straight — there are only two pages of questions left to go. Read the writing prompts below — oh, and at the risk of sounding like a broken record, don't forget to plan...

Your school is considering the advantages and disadvantages of using detentions as a punishment. They want you to write a speech arguing your viewpoint to deliver at the next school council meeting.

Your speech should include:

- your attitude towards the use of detentions as a punishment
- reasons why you hold this view, backed up with evidence
- reasons why others might disagree with you, followed by counter-arguments against these reasons

Write your speech for the school council.

10 marks

A local photographer has organised a writing competition on the theme of the sea. She has asked entrants to write a description of a setting, using the photograph below as inspiration. It should use lots of figurative language and reflect the atmosphere created in the photo.

Write your description based on the photograph.

10 marks

Your town's art club wants to produce an information leaflet for those interested in joining the group. Write a leaflet which provides useful information for potential new members.

Your information leaflet should include:

- a brief description of the art club's role in the community
- reasons why people should join the club
- a clear structure and layout

Write the text for this information leaflet.

10 marks

Section 11: Writing Review

Writing Review

A famous author is running a competition challenging the public to come up with a main character for his next novel. He would like entrants to write a character description about someone who is shy.

Your character description should include:

- a vivid description of your character's appearance
- a description of what the character says and does
- an exploration of your character's thoughts and feelings

Write your character description.

10 marks

Your local council is creating a new youth zone in your town and have asked for suggestions from young people about what amenities it should have. Write a letter to the council suggesting the type of facilities young people would like.

Your letter should include:

- suggestions for a variety of facilities in the youth zone
- reasons why you think they would be suitable
- evidence to support the reasons you have given

Write your letter.

10 marks

A magazine has asked its readers to submit stories for a creative writing section.

Calling all aspiring writers! We want your creative writing contributions for next month's edition. We would like you to write a story about a time when you celebrated something. Don't delay — submit your story now for a chance to see your writing in print.

Write a story about a celebration.

10 marks

Answers

Section 1: Reading — Audience and Purpose

Page 3 — Before you Start
1. a) People who are planning to travel by plane, but have not flown before.
    b) Any sensible answer, e.g. The extract explains what to do at an airport, and it gives details that people who have flown before would already know.
2. a) to inform
    b) Any sensible answer, e.g. The text uses facts rather than opinions for accuracy.
3. a) You should have underlined: "the 'American Dream': a lifestyle focused on ambition and material success that many Americans desired."
    b) "the harsh reality of life during the Great Depression of the 1930s"

Page 4 — Audience
1. a) Any sensible answer, e.g. Experts in the field of celestial navigation.
    b) Any sensible answer, e.g. It uses technical language and references events in the field of celestial navigation without explaining what happened.
2. a) Any sensible answer, e.g. The author uses formal language and a serious tone.
    b) Any sensible answer, e.g. The author uses a short introductory paragraph to state their objection to the demolition of the mansion, then uses separate paragraphs to detail their two main concerns about the demolition.
    c) Any sensible answer, e.g. Formal language is appropriate because the letter is addressed to a public figure that the letter-writer doesn't know personally. The writer's tone is appropriate because they are raising a serious complaint that questions a decision that has been made. The use of paragraphs to emphasise key points makes the writer's argument clear to the letter's recipient.
    d) Any sensible answer, e.g. I would use informal language and adopt a less serious tone. I would also encourage my friend to support my objections to the demolition, rather than directing my objections at the reader.

Page 5 — Purpose
1. a) rhetorical question: "how can you resist?"
    direct address: Any sensible answer e.g. "your daily life", "revitalise your mind and body", "or your money back", "at your fingertips", "how can you resist", "both you and your bank account"
    b) Any sensible answer, e.g. The rhetorical question "how can you resist?" is effective because it encourages the reader to answer the question in their own mind, persuading them that they should visit the hotel.
2. a) To inform and to persuade
    b) Any sensible answers, e.g. statistics, emotive language
    c) Any sensible answer, e.g. Using statistics makes the text seem reliable and well-informed, while emotive language makes the reader feel more strongly about the issue, persuading them to limit their social media use.

Page 6 — Context
1. a) Any sensible answer, e.g. The extract suggests that women were unable to make decisions for themselves because men held power over their lives.
    b) Any sensible answer, e.g. The author uses repetition and rhetorical questions to show that the narrator's husband has power over her. The narrator disagrees with her husband, but repeats the rhetorical question "what is one to do?" while explaining her objections. This suggests that the narrator believes there is nothing she can do to challenge her husband's decision.
2. a) Any sensible answer, e.g. The children were exploited to the point where work was all they knew, so they can't imagine a life without it.
    b) Any sensible answer, e.g. The narrator urges the children to be free but they respond "Leave us quiet in the dark of the coal-shadows". This suggests that they have become so accustomed to their lives in the mine that they don't want to venture into the unfamiliar world beyond the mine.
    c) Any sensible answer, e.g. To highlight how unnatural and damaging it is for children to be forced to work in mines. Barrett Browning suggests children should want to play freely in nature and sing as "thrushes do", but instead the children in the poem prefer to be left in the darkness of the mine. This suggests that their natural desire to be free has been suppressed.

Section 2: Reading — Non-Fiction Texts

Page 7 — Before you Start
1. a) i) You should have ticked: to inform
       ii) The text is providing factual information to educate the reader about black holes.
    b) i) Any sensible answer, e.g formal, neutral, serious
       ii) Any sensible answer.
    c) Light can't escape from black holes, so they're invisible to the human eye.
    d) Any sensible answer that includes the main points from the first paragraph of the text.

Page 8 — Finding Evidence in the Text
1. a) 1883
    b) "will set you back a fair few pennies"
    c) "a much-needed break from the Spanish sun"
    d) Any sensible answers that use the text to justify each adjective.
    e) i) Any sensible answers, e.g. "and what do you know", "good old Metro", "One thing's for sure"
       ii) Any sensible answer, e.g. This tone makes the text more friendly and approachable — it feels like a friend recommending a place to visit.

Page 9 — Making Inferences
1. a) Any sensible answer, e.g. They were a runner. They talk about "the track", "winning" medals and refer to it as having been their sport "over the course of the years".

b) Any sensible answer, e.g. No — they say they were "always running just a little bit behind everyone else" and describe how they "daydreamed" rather than listening in class.
c) They didn't have any time or energy because they had recently had twins.
d) Any sensible answer, e.g. I think it wasn't particularly positive. They say they sat on their own at school and valued alone time on the track because nobody could tease them there.
e) Any sensible answer, e.g. People had misconceptions about the author — they saw the author as someone motivated by the prizes that come with winning rather than as an athlete passionate about their sport and talent.
f) Any sensible answer, e.g. Yes, they talk about the "prize money" and "medals" they collected over the years.

Page 10 — Layout and Structure

1. a) i) You should have ticked: It poses a problem to the reader and offers a solution.
   ii) Each bullet point is made up of a rhetorical question and a response.
   b) Any sensible answer, e.g. Yes, it emphasises certain key words within the advert which would appeal to the intended audience of the text.
   c) Any two from e.g. bullet points, capitalisation, eye-catching bubble, centre alignment. They break up the information and highlight key elements of the text.
   d) Any sensible answer, e.g. The writer uses rhetorical questions to make the reader feel as though they are being asked the questions themselves.
   e) Any sensible answer, e.g. I think that the structure is very effective — it engages the reader before giving more specific detail about the job. The layout is strong too, but would perhaps be more effective if the information were a little more spaced out to make it easier to read.

Pages 11-12 — Language Techniques

1. a) "Chai the chimp", "sunny state", "sold for such a sizeable sum", "animal artist"
   It makes these parts of the text stand out and become more memorable.
   b) i) metaphor, personification, colloquial language
      ii) Any sensible answers.
2. a) Any sensible answer, e.g. "scaring me half to death", "engulfed by unrelenting dread", "incessant ache"
   b) Any sensible answer, e.g. It encourages the reader to empathise with the author. Describing their fear so vividly allows the reader to put themselves in the soldier's shoes and makes it easier for them to sympathise with their experiences.
3. a) i) You should have circled: oxymoron and alliteration
      ii) A: "clean every corner", "deafening silence", "stubborn spaces spotless"
      B: "butter will be bubbling", "bittersweet",
      C: "small crowd", "bold black bear", "definite possibility",
      D: "sparkling success", "organised chaos"
   b) i) Rhetorical questions are used. They directly address the reader and guide their thoughts.
      ii) Any sensible answer, e.g. Text A's purpose is to persuade people to buy a product, so it seeks to make a direct appeal to the audience. This is not the case in the others.
   c) i) "The delectable fusion of tangy lemon and caramel tones"
      ii) Any sensible answer, e.g. This sensory language makes the recipe sound really appealing and encourages the reader to make it.
   d) i) A and B
      ii) Any sensible answer, e.g. It makes text A more dynamic and engaging, grabbing the reader's attention. In text B, it is informative, providing a sound effect to listen out for when cooking.

Page 13 — Tone

1. a) i) Any two sensible adjectives, e.g. disappointed and angry
      ii) Any evidence from the text which demonstrates each chosen adjective.
      iii) Any sensible answer
      iv) Any sensible answer
2. a)

Text	Appropriate Tone
a fan letter	complimentary
a sympathy card	compassionate
an 'Agony Aunt' blog	advisory
a food nutrition label	informative
a protest speech	passionate
a diary entry	candid

Different combinations of answers also work, but each word should only be used once and should convey an appropriate tone for the text.

   b) Any sensible answers that convey the appropriate tone.

Page 14 — What You Think

1. a) Any sensible answer, e.g. The extract made me feel relaxed but also inspired. It made me eager to travel.
   b) i) Any sensible answer, e.g. The author uses lots of language related to peace and tranquillity.
      ii) Any sensible answer, e.g. It makes the reader want to share the same experiences as the writer. The juxtaposition of this peaceful scene and hectic daily life at home is effective, as it makes the reader compare their own lifestyle with the writer's travels.
   c) Any sensible answer, e.g. The writer begins to use imperative sentences and a more authoritative tone. This helps to motivate the reader.
   d) Any sensible answers, e.g.

Quote	Effect
"the intense pulse of fierce heat on my back"	This vivid and striking description using sensory language makes the reader almost able to feel the sun's heat.
"This town breathes peace and serenity"	This personification emphasises that calmness is at the town's core, making the location sound very appealing.
"such freedom in being offbeat"	This motivates the reader, inspiring them to follow the author's advice.

e) Any sensible answer, e.g. Yes, the author has provided the reader with information and detail about the location, but they have also persuaded the reader to come around to their way of thinking. They have made taking "the road less travelled" seem appealing and inspiring.

Page 15 — The Author's Intentions
1 a) Other protesters or individuals with similar views
   b) You should have circled: to persuade
   c) Any sensible answer, e.g. The full stops in "Every. Single. Year." create dramatic pauses to emphasise the words to the audience and focus their attention on the author's point.
   d) You should have ticked: It forces the reader to imagine the animals' experiences.
   e) Any sensible answer, e.g. The author's tone is passionate — the strength of their conviction would help to persuade others to feel the same way.
   f) Any two examples, e.g. "physical suffering", "harrowing". The author uses emotive language to appeal to the reader's conscience and encourage the audience to empathise with the animals.
   g) Any sensible answer, e.g. Yes, I agree. The author uses statistics to support their argument, which inspires confidence in their view and makes them seem like an authority on the issue. They also use imperatives, commanding the audience to take action.

Section 3: Reading — Fiction and Plays

Page 16 — Before you Start
1 a) You should have circled: amusing
   b) E.g. "But your name is Ernest."
   c) Any sensible answer, e.g. Gwendolen finds the name boring and uninspiring. The audience might find this amusing because they know that Ernest's real name is Jack.
   d) Any sensible answer, e.g. Yes, because Gwendolen decides to love Ernest because of his name. She tells Ernest that her "ideal" is to love someone called Ernest, and implies that she couldn't love Ernest if he had another name. This makes Gwendolen seem superficial because she bases a big decision about her life on something as trivial as a name.

Page 17 — Finding Evidence in the Text
1 a) She had an extra 15 minutes of sleep.
   b) Any sensible answers, e.g.
   stressed: "tapped her foot impatiently", "silently urged"
   hot: "The summer was taking its toll", "a bead of sweat trickled down her face"
   nervous: "trembling hands"
   agile: "she weaved in and out of the market crowds like a needle pulling thread"
   c) i) They are compared to a monster and a swarm of insects.
      ii) Any sensible answer, e.g. It suggests that Lauren sees the crowds as something massive and unbeatable, but also mindless and irritating creatures that are in her way.
   d) Any sensible answer, e.g. Yes, Lauren seems like a conscientious and diligent character. She scales "the escalator in unflinching strides" and runs through crowds to get to work on time. When she arrives, she has "trembling hands" and wonders whether she has "done it". This all suggests she feels a sense of guilt for not being punctual.

Page 18 — Making Inferences
1 a) E.g. "You ready?", "Okay. Inhale."
   b) Any sensible answers, e.g.

Quote from the extract	Inference
"This book, this actual book, is set right *here*, on Earth."	This narrator is not from Earth — most wouldn't need to clarify this point.
"It is, in short, about how to become a human."	The narrator is writing to educate their audience.

   c) i) Someone who is not human.
      ii) Any sensible answer, e.g. The narrator thinks it could be the first time the reader has encountered human "written language", and the narrator states that their reader has an "instantaneous ability" to translate "primitive linguistic forms". This suggests that the narrator is addressing someone with inhuman abilities who isn't familiar with human society.
   d) i) Any sensible answer, e.g. The narrator suggests that being human is a very confusing, but wonderful experience. They sum up being human in a list that includes a series of opposing ideas, such as "the meaning of life and nothing at all", and random elements of human life like "wholenut peanut butter". This suggests that being human involves lots of contradictions, but it also involves moments of random joy.
      ii) Any sensible answer, e.g. Yes, because while the narrator's summary of humans includes negative elements like "hate" and the idea that humans sometimes need saving, the summary has an almost awestruck tone, suggesting that the narrator appreciates the randomness and richness of the humans that he is describing.

Page 19 — Structure
1 a) Any sensible answer, e.g. The author repeats the phrase "I see the world a little differently". This repetition reinforces the suggestion that there is much more to the narrator's story than the reader knows so far.
   b) Any sensible answer, e.g. the voice inside the first narrator's head
   c) i) Any sensible answer, e.g. The text is structured like a back-and-forth interaction between the first narrator and their inner thoughts. It jumps back and forth between two obviously different 'voices' quite sporadically, with interruptions from the 'thoughts'. This makes it clear that these are two different perspectives.
      ii) Any sensible answer, e.g. Yes. It is interesting because it is surprising to read a text with two voices that effectively come from the same character. I think it is an unusual structural technique which intrigues the reader and makes them want to read on.

d) Any sensible answer, e.g. The author uses the back-and-forth argument between the narrator and their thoughts to create humour. The interruptions, disagreements and irritable comments are amusing for the reader.

e) Any sensible answer, e.g. The chatty structure implies that the narrator might be lonely as they have in-depth conversations with their thoughts, the only "company" they have.

Page 20 — Themes

1. a) E.g. "I was a captive and a slave."

   b) Any sensible answer, e.g. The word "headlong" suggests that David falls in love quickly and recklessly, while the word "abyss" suggests that David's love is deep and unending.

   c) i) You should have ticked: Love can be all-consuming.

   ii) Any sensible answer, e.g. Dickens uses David's description of falling in love with Dora to emphasise the all-consuming nature of love. In the extract, David states that he loved Dora "to distraction", which suggests that he is unable to think of anything other than her, while the imagery of David falling into an "abyss of love" suggests that he has fallen so deeply and totally in love with Dora that he has no hope of escaping his feelings.

2. a) Any sensible answer, e.g. It suggests that he values her highly and that she is precious to him.

   b) Any sensible answer, e.g. Rochester tells Jane he would love her even if her mind were "broken" and would show her "untiring tenderness" even if she no longer recognised him. This suggests that love involves hardships as well as joy.

3. Any sensible similarities or differences that are supported with evidence from the text, e.g. David and Rochester are both devoted to the person they love. Rochester claims he would love Jane even if she "had no longer a ray of recognition" for him, suggesting that he will love her no matter what happens. David claims to love Dora "to distraction", suggesting that he thinks of nothing else but loving her. However, while David idealises Dora, calling her a "Fairy" and talking of loving her at first sight, Rochester seems to have a more mature understanding of love and devotion. He seems to know more about Jane and recognises that love can face, and withstand, real challenges.

Page 21 — Language Techniques

1. a) i) One of: "what light through yonder window breaks?" **Or** "what of that?" **Or** "What if her eyes were there, they in her head?"

   ii) Any sensible answer, e.g. It suggests Romeo is so captivated by Juliet that he can hardly believe she is real.

   b) i) Two of: "fair sun", "kill the envious moon", "she is envious", "Who is already sick and pale with grief", "Her vestal livery is but sick and green"

   ii) Any sensible answer that explains the effect of each example of personification on the reader.

   c) Any sensible answer, e.g. Shakespeare uses figurative language to compare Juliet to images of light, and particularly the Sun. This suggests she is hugely important to Romeo as she is his light.

   d) Any sensible answer, e.g. Shakespeare writes that Juliet's eyes could "twinkle" in place of the stars.

This emphasises how bright her eyes are, which makes her sound radiantly beautiful. He repeats the idea that she is radiant saying she would "shame" the stars like "daylight doth a lamp". Comparing her to "daylight" suggests that Juliet's beauty lights up his entire world.

Pages 22-23 — Characterisation

1. a) i) Ofelia's father seems **warm** in the extract.
   E.g. "his voice soft with tenderness"

   ii) Ofelia uses books to **escape from** her life.
   E.g. "the words they offered granted shelter and comfort"

   b) Any sensible answer, e.g. "she didn't want to think about him."

   c) Any sensible answer, e.g. It suggests that Ofelia's mother has been hurt and damaged. The fact that her voice was musical like a bell, but is now broken, suggests she's lost her joy and liveliness.

   d) Any sensible answer, e.g. The author writes of them driving "farther and farther away from everything Ofelia knew" to emphasise her physical remoteness. Ofelia seems surrounded by people who don't understand her, like her mother and stepfather, but far away from those who do, like her loving father. This suggests she is feeling both physically and emotionally isolated.

   e) Any sensible answer, e.g No, because she hasn't lost hope. She may be struggling with her current situation, but she still finds solace in books and memories, which suggests she still manages to find small pockets of joy in hard times.

2. a) You should have ticked: frustrated
   Any sensible answer, e.g. "*Travis jabs his spoon into his cereal bowl viciously*"

   b) Any sensible answer, e.g. Yes, even though Ruth repeatedly tells him to stop asking about the "fifty cents", he badgers her, suggesting different ways he could go about getting the money.

   c) Any sensible answer, e.g. Ruth uses imperative phrases like "Hush up now" and "Come here" to order Travis to behave, as well as using his name multiple times to assert authority. She repeatedly scolds him when he answers back, which makes him weaken at the end of the extract, where he begins merely saying "I'm gone" in response to her lectures and fussing. This shows that she has the power in the relationship.

   d) Any sensible answer, e.g. I think they are similar, which is why they seem to clash. Neither character concedes in the argument, which suggests that they are both stubborn. Hansberry writes that "*They are both quiet and tense for several seconds*" which makes them both seem headstrong, but also suggests that neither likes arguing. However, Travis removes himself from the situation — "I'm gone" — which shows that they have a different approach to confrontation.

Pages 24-25 — Setting

1. a) i) "the lodge-gates, a maze of fantastic tracery in wrought iron"

   ii) "The lodge was a ruin of black granite and bared ribs of rafters"

   b) Any sensible answer, e.g. Conan Doyle refers to bright colours, such as "gold" and "red", at the start of the extract. As the journey continues, he refers to darker, more muted colours like "russet" and "olive", before referring to the "black" ruins on the Baskerville estate. The darkening of the colours reflects the atmosphere becoming gradually wilder, more mysterious and more sinister.

- c) Any sensible answer, e.g. Conan Doyle creates an eeriness to the building by comparing it to "a ghost". He introduces the idea that the setting might be frightening or unsettling. Likening Baskerville Hall to something supernatural suggests it is unearthly, adding to the sense of foreboding.
- d) i) You should have ticked: unsettling
  ii) Any sensible answer, e.g. The author creates an unsettling atmosphere by building an unruly and sinister picture of nature as the carriage approaches the hall. He refers to the unnatural shapes of storm-twisted firs and "stunted oaks", which creates a sinister atmosphere. He also describes how their approach was "hushed amid the leaves", which seems quite menacing, alongside the fact that trees enclosed them in a "sombre tunnel".

2 a) Any sensible answer, e.g. The author compares the setting to soup, a food that is usually related to comfort, but uses strong, violent verbs and adjectives like "boiling" and "burned" to make the atmosphere seem threatening and dangerous.
- b) Any sensible answer, e.g. The juxtaposition of these two opposing sounds shocks the reader, highlighting how quickly the setting changes from something happy to something horrifying.
- c) The author has used a metaphor. Any sensible explanation, e.g. Zusak uses this violent imagery to refer to the bombing as having caused a serious injury. This emphasises the effect of the bombing on the town itself, and also refers to the blood spilt by all the human casualties.
- d) Any sensible answer, e.g. In the first extract, the atmosphere is very obviously distressing and dangerous. Zusak refers to "Blood" streaming and bodies "like driftwood", which creates a harrowing scene. In the second extract, however, the setting seems a bit more still. The author uses peaceful and serene language like "Snowflakes of ash" to reflect a quieter, less dangerous atmosphere. Despite this, the writer still uses lots of imagery related to destruction like "devastating", "flung apart" and "scorched". This suggests that although the actual bombing has come to an end, the extent of the destruction and human cost is still extremely clear.

Pages 26-27 — Interpreting Plays

1 a) Any sensible answer, e.g. She might feel distrusted as Danforth accuses her of being deceitful.
- b) 1 — Mary admits she didn't see spirits.
  2 — Parris doubts Mary's claim and tries to influence Danforth.
  3 — Danforth asks Abigail if she definitely saw spirits.
  4 — Abigail threatens Danforth.
  5 — Abigail and Mercy seem to experience something supernatural.
- c) i) E.g. "Surely Your Excellency is not taken by this simple lie."
  ii) "to God every soul is precious"
- d) Any sensible answer, e.g. The hesitation suggests that Mary is feeling anxious. She stutters on her words, which indicates that she is distressed and unnerved by the situation.
- e) Any sensible answer, e.g. The atmosphere at the beginning of the extract feels tense and combative as it begins with a dispute. By the end, the atmosphere becomes darker and much more chilling when it is suggested that the girls might be affected by witchraft.
- f) Any sensible answer, e.g. Yes, because he questions Abigail and Mercy, which suggests he sees some potential truth in the claim.
- g) Any sensible answer, e.g. The playwright structures the scene as an interrogation in which the characters all interject at various times. This confusion means that the reader might not know who Danforth will believe, as he seems to waver between trusting them both with each interruption — they don't know what will happen next.
- h) Any sensible answer, e.g. Yes, she uses emotive language — "I done my duty...and this is my reward?" — to manipulate Danforth into sympathising with her. She also threatens Danforth, "Let *you* beware, Mr Danforth", and uses religion to try to manipulate his decisions, as she knows he is godfearing. Her acting towards the end of the extract also serves to manipulate the room into being suspicious of Mary Warren.
- i) Any sensible answer, e.g. I think that Abigail and Mercy are pretending to have a surreal experience at the end of the extract. The girls object to Mary's accusations against them, and seem to take the opportunity to frame her. Abigail's eyes *"fall on Mary Warren"* as she claims to feel "a cold wind", and Mary's *"terrified, pleading"* reaction to this suggests that she knows that Abigail is trying to frame her.

Page 28 — Staging and Performance

1 a) Any sensible answer, e.g. At the beginning of the extract, Macbeth believes the dagger is real, but gradually comes to understand that it is a hallucination as the text goes on. He then questions whether he can see it as the act of murder is on his mind. Macbeth appears quite aware of his own emotional and mental state, despite having this hallucination.
- b) i) Any three sensible answers, e.g.

Quotation	How could the actor speak and move?
"Is this a dagger which I see before me"	The actor could reach out into the air, perhaps pausing throughout the line to suggest disbelief.
"Come, let me clutch thee. / I have thee not"	The actor could start grabbing the air repeatedly, maybe becoming a little annoyed.
"on thy blade and dudgeon gouts of blood"	The actor could retreat from the dagger, and use pauses and facial expressions to show disgust.

  ii) Any sensible answer.

c) Any sensible answer, e.g. I would not stage the dagger's presence because it might be difficult for the audience to work out that it is a hallucination rather than reality. I think Macbeth should reach out for the air in front of him while speaking about the dagger, so it is clear that he can see a weapon, but nobody else can.

Pages 29 — What You Think
1 a) i) You should have circled: curious
   ii) Any sensible answer, e.g. Yes, because you would expect the narrator to be afraid of all the frightening features of the house and its owner.
   b) Any sensible answer, e.g. The ominous sounds create a vivid impression of eeriness, which makes the reader feel on edge.
   c) Any sensible answer, e.g. It makes the greeting seem like a ritual, and the reader questions why the narrator entering of his "own will" is so important. It implies something dangerous might be waiting for the narrator inside.
   d) Any sensible answer, e.g. The setting feels quite foreboding and menacing. Stoker's description of the "great door", and reference to it not having been used for a long while, suggests that something sinister is waiting inside, and this makes the reader nervous, but also keen to read on.
   e) Any sensible answer, e.g. The description of the old man is unsettling. At the start of the extract, the narrator observes that there is not "a single speck of colour" on the old man, which makes him seem cold and a little sinister. The author later uses the simile "as cold as ice" to describe the old man's touch, and compares his hand to that of a "dead" man. This is unnerving because it confirms the sinister impression of the old man that was created at the start of the extract.

Section 4: Reading — Poetry

Page 30 — Before you Start
1 a) i) You should have ticked: life
   ii) Any sensible answer, e.g. The road is an extended metaphor for life because the poem suggests that the road can change its course — that life can change and people don't know what their life will bring. In the poem, it's the road that decides to change, not the traveller. The poem also suggests that the reader must follow the road "without knowing what's on the other side", reflecting the fact that people rarely know how their life will unfold.
   b) Any sensible answer, e.g. The poet uses rhetorical questions to encourage the reader to think about the ideas in the poem.
   c) Any sensible answer, e.g. The poet does this to show that the road is not fixed in place and can adjust to changes, like cloth takes the shape of what's beneath it.
   d) Any sensible answer, e.g. The narrator suggests that feeling uncertain about the future is positive. They ask the reader "who wants to know a story's end", which implies that life's unpredictability and mystery should be celebrated as an exciting concept, rather than feared.

Page 31 — Making Inferences
1 a) a hill
   b) Any sensible answer, e.g. I think it suggests that the narrator did not realise they were in the prime of their life at the time. They were oblivious to this until they passed it, only then realising they had forgotten to rejoice in it.
   c) Any sensible answer, e.g. I think the narrator is feeling regretful and disappointed. They spent a lot of time idealising the experience of reaching the "crest", imagining feeling a sense of pride, but it didn't stand out and was underwhelming when it materialised.
   d) Any sensible answer, e.g. I think the brambles symbolise difficulties in life that distract the narrator from appreciating the best parts of their life.
   e) Any sensible answer, e.g. The narrator has experienced the best moments of life. Now they are over, there is no way things can improve — the only way is down.

Page 32 — Structure
1 a) i) You should have circled: free verse
   ii) Any sensible answer, e.g. The poet chose free verse so they could have more freedom over the poem's rhyme and rhythm. It makes the poem sound more like speech, as though she is directly speaking to her mother.
   b) Any sensible answer, e.g. The lack of punctuation allows the lines and stanzas to flow into each other smoothly, which helps to create a sense of momentum as the narrator gives more and more reasons to praise her mother.
   c) Any sensible answer, e.g. The poet uses repetition to create a sense of momentum and growth in the poem. For example, the narrator repeats the structure "You were / [X] to me" at the start of the stanzas to gradually build up an image of the importance of their mother. She also repeats the word "replenishing" immediately after itself to reflect the comforting smell of her mother's cooking constantly renewing.
   d) Any sensible answer, e.g. Within each of the first four stanzas, the lines increase in length, particularly in the fourth stanza which ends with a much longer line. The fourth stanza is also longer than the previous three. This create a sense of growth throughout the poem, which reflects how the narrator's mother opens up wider possibilities to her daughter in the last stanza.
   e) Any sensible answer, e.g. I think the last line is on its own because it is different in form to the other stanzas. The first stanzas describe the narrator's fondness for her mother in a reasonably regular form. Whereas, the last stanza deviates sharply from the form because it begins from her mother's perspective instead. Putting the final line in its own stanza makes it stand out and helps reflect the fact that it is a very broad, open statement.

Page 33 — Themes
1 a) Any sensible answer, e.g. It suggests that the narrator feels strongly about London, as it triggers a sudden feeling of excitement in them.
   b) Any sensible answer, e.g. The River Thames, red buses and tube trains are all instantly recognisable

Answers

icons of London. Comparing their thoughts to these features reflects the narrator's strong connection to the city as a key part of their identity.

c) i) You should have ticked: It makes the poem flow steadily.
   ii) Any sensible answer, e.g. The natural flow of the lines reflects how the narrator's love for London comes naturally and easily. The flowing lines indicate that the poem could go on forever, just like their love will.

d) Any sensible answer, e.g. The metaphor of the narrator as London's "child" reflects the strong bond and close attachment they have with the city, as if London were their parent and made them who they are.

Page 34 — Voice

1 a) i) Any three examples of phonetic spelling, e.g. "mi", "lef" and "diffrun"
      ii) Any sensible answer, e.g. They suggest that the narrator is Jamaican as the phonetic spellings represent how the words would sound in a Jamaican accent.
   b) i) Any sensible answer, e.g. hopeful but desperate
      ii) The use of "this lickle luck" and "this lickle light" creates an increasingly hopeful tone towards the end of the poem, as the narrator sees a way out of their situation. However, the poem also has a tone of desperation because the narrator seems willing to do anything to escape their homeland, even if it is immoral: they would "hurt" and "cheat or lie" to get on the ship.
      iii) Any sensible answer, e.g. The poem's tone suggests that the narrator is a determined and optimistic character. They are determined to get on the ship by whatever method possible, because they believe that it will change their life for the better.
   c) Any sensible answer, e.g. No, I don't think they want to leave their heritage completely. Although the narrator is desperate to "travel this ship", Berry's use of phonetic spellings throughout the poem, which echoes the narrator's Jamaican accent, suggests that they are proud of their heritage.

Page 35 — Techniques

1 a) i) Any sensible answer, e.g. Cats are very flexible and move smoothly, like liquid.
      ii) Any sensible answer, e.g. Enjambment makes the lines flow smoothly, which reflects the smooth, flowing movement of the cats.
   b) "obsequious as darkness"
      Any sensible answer, e.g. Darkness doesn't follow any human rules. Therefore, the simile suggests that cats are very disobedient, coming and going as they please instead of following their owner's rules.
   c) Any sensible answer, e.g. The negative phrasing reflects the cats' disobedient nature. They do not do as they are told, and they are uncooperative with both humans and natural forces such as the wind.
   d) Any sensible answer, e.g. The poet suggests the constant movement of cats by using lots of verbs to describe their actions throughout the poem, such as "slip" and "twist". The pair of adjectives "diminished, neat" describes the amazing ability of cats to squeeze into impossible spaces. This quality is reinforced by the repetition of the image "no less liquid than their shadows" at the start and end of the extract. The unpredictability of cats is emphasised by the alliteration of "r" and repetition in the line "Quick to retire, quick to return", which suggests that cats do whatever they want whenever they please.

Pages 36-37 — Interpreting Poems

1 a) Any sensible answer, e.g. The poem is about a violent storm on the beach in the middle of the night.
   b) Any sensible answer, e.g. People who are patrolling the beach.
   c) You should have underlined:
      "slush and sand spirts of snow fierce slanting", "swirl and spray", "Slush and sand" and "Steadily, slowly"
      Any sensible explanation of one of these, e.g. The sibilance in the phrase "swirl and spray" imitates the sound of the water being swirled by the wind and spraying into the air.
   d) i) The rhythm is irregular and sporadic.
      ii) Any sensible answer, e.g. The random stresses mirror the storm's chaos and unpredictable nature. The use of the "ing" sound at the end of every line pushes the rhythm on and helps create a sense of constant movement.
   e) Any sensible answer, e.g. Nature appears to be incredibly powerful and threatening in this poem. This impression is created by the poet's use of personification in the description of the storm "muttering" and shouting with "demoniac laughter". This makes the storm seem to be alive and makes its violent actions, such as "lashing" the beach, seem deliberate and cruel. Nature also seems dangerous, as the poet describes the gale as a "death-wind", and calls the combination of waves, air and midnight "savage".
   f) Any sensible answer, e.g. The tone is intense and wild. This makes the reader feel frightened and overwhelmed by the power and ferocity of the storm.

2 a) You should have ticked:
      The narrator's misery is making it difficult for them to complete daily tasks.
   b) i) Any sensible answer, e.g. The poet uses lots of exclamation marks coupled with pauses in the lines, making the stanza seem frantic and frenzied.
      ii) The narrator is struggling to live with their pain, becoming distressed with life as a result.
   c) Any sensible answer, e.g. The poem constantly repeats "Love has gone and left me", suggesting that loneliness has caused the narrator's misery. Repeating this line emphasises the narrator's persistent feelings of isolation, and incapability of shaking their sadness.
   d) Any sensible answer, e.g. The narrator is comparing life to something that is relentlessly chipping away at them, gradually making them weaker and weaker. It suggests that life is simply irritating to the narrator.
   e) Any sensible answer, e.g. I think the narrator doesn't see any end to their sadness, as the poet repeats "to-morrow", emphasising the repetitiveness and recurrence of their days to come. They diminish their life as merely a "little street and this little house", suggesting their life will remain tedious and spiritless.

Page 38 — Comparing Poems

1. a) i) both
      ii) Farewell
      iii) Ashes of Life
   b) Any sensible summary, e.g. Both narrators have suffered loss, but they react differently to it. In 'Ashes of Life', the narrator sees no respite from their pain so their life is effectively in "Ashes", whereas in 'Farewell', the narrator is grateful for the love that they had, despite their pain.
   c) i) E.g. "all my thousand prayers"
      ii) In 'Farewell', Brontë uses figurative language to describe the beauty of the partner, whereas in 'Ashes of Life', Millay uses figurative language to express the constancy of the narrator's pain. Brontë's image of the partner's "laughing eye" suggests that despite loss, the narrator's memories of the person are buoyant and bright. Brontë also indicates the extent of the narrator's love for their partner, using a metaphor to describe an "echo" in them triggered merely by the person's voice. In contrast, Millay uses a simile to describe how their pain-filled existence is like a relentless and frustrating "gnawing". Millay also uses personification to describe love as having "gone and left me", suggesting love is a cruel and ruthless thing that has deserted the narrator.
   d) Any sensible answer, e.g. The poets use similar forms, but they reflect different ideas. Millay's use of 4-line stanzas and a regular ABAB rhyme scheme mirrors the monotony and repetitiveness of her pain. Whereas, Brontë's 4-line stanzas and regular ABAB rhyme scheme reflects the sense of balance and completeness the narrator has found in the relationship.
   e) Any sensible answer, e.g. The poems differ substantially in tone. The narrator of 'Farewell' has a positive tone, praising their partner as "beautiful", "joyous" and "magic". In contrast, the narrator of 'Ashes of Life' has a much more negative tone, repeatedly describing their lost love as having "left" them and complaining that life is pointless. The stark difference in tone between the poems highlights to the reader that people respond to loss in different ways.
   f) Any three sensible paragraphs, e.g.
      The poets present loss as an experience that provokes intense emotion. They both use exclamatory lines: Millay's narrator dismally exclaims "But ah! — to lie awake and hear the slow hours strike!", whilst Brontë's narrator exclaims fondly "O, beautiful, and full of grace!", suggesting that their loss just made them view their love more positively and intensely. These exclamations suggest that while the two narrators reflect on loss in wildly different ways, they both experience it passionately.

Section 5: Reading — Comparing Texts

Page 39 — Before you Start

1. a) Any sensible sentences that summarise the main idea of each text, e.g. A is an account in which the narrator discovers an unfamiliar animal. Text B is a newspaper article about a feather discovered in a forest

   b) i) Any sensible answer, e.g. The narrator is intrigued by the creature and its unusual features, like its "scales and bony thorns", but they are also "unnerved" by it.
      ii) Any sensible answer, e.g. Unlike in Text A, the reaction to the discovery in Text B is completely positive. The town is "abuzz" with the news of the feather and everyone is excited about the "staggering" and "earth-shattering" discovery.
   c) Any sensible comparison of the language used in both texts.
   d) Any sensible answer, e.g. Text A is structured more narratively, following the process of finding the animal from beginning to end. Text B begins with the news that something rare has been found — this captures the reader's attention. It is then followed by commentary about the discovery.

Pages 41-43 — Comparing Texts

1. Any sensible summaries that cover the main points of each text, e.g.
   An archaeologist studying ancient Mayan ruins gets lost in the middle of the rainforest.
   An estate agent shows potential buyers around a perfectly presented building that has some secrets lying beneath the surface.
   The narrator dreams of returning to a place they once knew, but the grounds are now dilapidated and overgrown.

2.
	The Mayan Expedition	The Mystery of Camel Manor	Rebecca
It uses direct speech.		x	
The narrator imagines the events in the extract.			x
It uses sensory language to describe rock.	x		
It uses figurative language to describe trees.			x

3. nature's destructive power — *Rebecca*
   subduing nature's power — *The Mystery of Camel Manor*
   secrets hidden by nature — *The Mayan Expedition*

4. Any sensible answer, e.g. Its purpose is to keep a record of the expedition, rather than to entertain.

5. a) Any sensible answer, e.g. The central road and paths in the jungle are compared to a snake slithering through the trees.
   b) E.g. "The drive was a ribbon now, a thread of its former self", "the poor thread that had once been our drive"
   c) Any sensible answer, e.g. I think the metaphor in *Rebecca* is the most effective, as it creates a more interesting and unusual picture in the reader's mind.

6. a) Any sensible answer, e.g. unconvincing
      The estate agent launches into a number of lengthy descriptions of the house, but the narrator is sceptical of her because it sounds very rehearsed. Despite her best efforts to persuade the narrator, they are not convinced.
   b) Any sensible answer, e.g. The estate agent's tone is very formal, using complex vocabulary to describe the house. The narrator's tone in *The Mayan Expedition* is also formal and informative, using technical language throughout to describe the discovery.

7   Any sensible answer, e.g. The narrator in *The Mystery of Camel Manor* is seeing "an immaculately presented building" that is clean and polished, but empty of character. Alternatively, the narrator in *Rebecca* is returning to a place that was once beautiful but the impact of nature has meant "a change had come upon it". Where the narrator experiences the house falling into disrepair in *Rebecca*, the house is perfectly restored in *The Mystery of Camel Manor*.

8 a)   Any sensible answer, e.g. "her stealthy, insidious way had encroached...with long, tenacious fingers" Daphne du Maurier uses personification to portray nature as cunning, deliberately damaging Manderley out of spite rather than because it is a natural process that occurs over time.

  b)   Any sensible answer, e.g. "This main façade was once choked by a sprawling mass of persistent ivy" In *The Mystery of Camel Manor*, the writer also portrays nature as an uncontrollable and negative force. The image of choking is disturbing, and suggests that nature was holding this building's potential beauty hostage until it could be successfully restored.

9 a)   Any sensible answer, e.g. I think it is portrayed as powerful, but I don't think it is threatening. The narrator struggles with the concept of "the boundless ecosystem" and "the searing heat", but perceives it as something to respect rather than be threatened by — they reflect on the unfortunate loss of harmony between humans and nature. The metaphor "leafy embrace" is also more of a comforting image which portrays nature as a dominant power, but warm and respectful.

  b)   Any sensible comparison of the presentation of nature that uses evidence from both texts.

10   Any sensible comparison of structure and form that uses evidence from both texts, e.g. *The Mayan Expedition* is a journal, so the information is structured in chronological order, presented in paragraphs for each entry. Alternatively, *Rebecca* is structured as a long descriptive account of a place, with little order.

11   Any sensible comparison of setting and atmosphere that uses evidence from both texts, e.g. The descriptions of setting in *Rebecca* creates an eerie and bleak atmosphere through dismal images like "tortured elms" and "gnarled roots", suggesting the place is unsettling and dangerous. The setting in *The Mayan Expedition* is more impressive, as the narrator describes being awestruck by the discovery of the temple. The narrator uses adverbs like "remarkably", "astonishingly" and "astoundingly" which suggests they are stunned by their discovery, but also by the sheer beauty of it.

12   Any sensible comparison of tone that considers the effect on the reader.

Section 6: Reading Review

Page 45 — Reading Review

1   Any sensible summary, e.g. Victor's attempt to bring a body to life succeeds *[1 mark]*. However, Victor is horrified at his creation and leaves the room, before going to sleep *[1 mark]*. He has a nightmare and when he wakes the creature is by his bed, so he runs outside in fear *[1 mark]*.

2 a)   Any sensible answer, e.g. "infusing life into an inanimate body" *[1 mark]*

  b)   Any sensible answer, e.g. It is surprising because the noun "catastrophe" implies that the experiment was a failure *[1 mark]* but the experiment was a success: the body came to life. *[1 mark]*

3 a)   Any sensible answer, e.g. The atmosphere is dark and gloomy. *[1 mark]*

  b)   Any sensible explanation, e.g. The extract's setting reinforces this atmosphere because it takes place "on a dreary night of November", with rain pattering "dismally" against the windows *[1 mark]*. This implies that it is dark and bleak outside, while the descriptions "dreary" and "dismally" highlight the gloomy mood *[1 mark]*.

4 a)   Any sensible answer, e.g. He was very passionate about his work and utterly dedicated to it *[1 mark]*.

  b)   Any sensible answer, e.g. His enthusiasm instantly turns to fear and revulsion when the creature comes to life *[1 mark]*. This is because Victor imagined that his creation would be beautiful, but he now believes that it is monstrous *[1 mark]*.

  c)   You should have used details from the text to explain how Shelley uses language to emphasise Victor's feelings in this part of the extract.
1-2 marks for a simple answer that uses some detail from the text to explain how Shelley uses language to emphasise Victor's feelings.
3-4 marks for a well-developed answer that uses detail from the text to clearly explain how Shelley uses language to emphasise Victor's feelings.
Here is an example of a point you may have made: Shelley contrasts Victor's previous "ardour" with his feelings of "breathless horror and disgust" when the experiment works. The pair of emotive adjectives "horror and disgust" highlight the strength of Victor's feelings. Towards the end of the paragraph, Victor describes the creature as a "demoniacal corpse". By comparing the creature to a demon, Shelley emphasises Victor's horror at what he has done as it makes the creature sound evil.

5   You should have used details from the text to explain the significance of Victor's nightmare.
1-2 marks for a simple answer that uses some detail from the text to explain the significance of the nightmare.
3-4 marks for a well-developed answer that uses detail from the text to clearly explain the significance of the nightmare.
Here is an example of a point you may have made: The nightmare reflects Victor's horror at what he has done. The unnatural image of Elizabeth becoming "livid with the hue of death" when Victor kisses her reverses the unnatural process of Victor bringing a dead body to life. The nightmare also adds to the mood of terror in the extract. The description of Elizabeth transforming into a "corpse" of Frankenstein's mother, full of crawling "grave-worms" is frightening and revolting.

6   You should have used details from the text to explain how Shelley makes the creature seem monstrous.
1-3 marks for a simple answer that uses some details from the text to explain how Shelley makes the creature seem monstrous.

4-6 marks for a well-developed answer that is supported by details from the text to clearly explain how Shelley makes the creature seem monstrous.

Here are some points and explanations you might have included:
- Victor describes the "beautiful" features of the creature, such as his "lustrous" and "flowing" hair, which Shelley contrasts with ugly, dead-looking features such as his "watery eyes" and "shrivelled complexion". This contrast highlights the creature's monstrosity.
- Shelley describes Victor being horrified by the creature in detail. Victor's disgust is suggested by his description of the creature as a "wretch", and his attempts to run away from it.
- Shelley makes the creature seem like a beast rather than a human. For example, instead of speaking, the creature can only make "inarticulate sounds".

7 You should have used details from the text to explain how Shelley makes the extract frightening, referring to language and structure.
1-3 marks for a simple answer that uses some details from the text to explain how Shelley uses language and structure to make the extract frightening.
4-6 marks for a well-developed answer that is supported by details from the text to explain how Shelley uses language and structure to make the extract frightening.
7-8 marks for a very developed answer that is well-supported by details from the text to clearly explain how Shelley uses language and structure to make the extract frightening.
- The extract begins by creating a dark and frightening atmosphere through Shelley's description of the setting. The extract takes place on a "dreary night", with the rain falling "dismally".
- Shelley describes Victor's terrified reaction in detail, making the creature seem monstrous. Its monstrousness is increased by the "horrid contrast" between its "beautiful" features and its "shrivelled complexion".
- Shelley vividly describes Victor's terror. For example, he paces around in "the greatest agitation" at the end of the extract, "fearing each sound" because it could mean the monster is approaching.
- Shelley uses a first-person narrator to emphasise Victor's fear. This makes the reader feel frightened, as it makes the extract seem more immediate.
- Shelley's description of Victor's nightmare makes the extract frightening because it uses horrific imagery. Victor's delight at dreaming of Elizabeth turns to "horror" as she decomposes into the corpse of his dead mother, covered in "grave-worms".
- The extract is frightening because it seems like there is no way to escape the creature. Even though Victor runs away from him, he finds the monster by his bed, and at the end of the extract there is a sense that he could be lurking just around the corner.

Page 47 — Reading Review

1 Any sensible summary, e.g. A water pipe bursts so everyone rushes to collect the water and children play in the spray *[1 mark]*.

2 a) "The skin cracks like a pod" *[1 mark]*
   b) Any sensible answer, e.g. The simile suggests that the poem is set somewhere hot and dry, as it refers to the suffering associated with not having enough water to drink *[2 marks]*.

3 a) Any three out of: "cracks", "drip", "splash", "echo", "rush", "roar", "crashes" *[1 mark for three words]*
   b) Any sensible answer, e.g. Onomatopoeia brings the sounds of the poem to life by making the reader hear them *[1 mark]*. This makes the events of the poem vivid, as the reader can hear the sound of the water rushing and the people's reactions *[1 mark]*.

4 Any sensible answer, e.g. Water is described as "silver" in the third stanza *[1 mark]*. This makes water seem very valuable and precious, as silver is an expensive metal *[1 mark]*.

5 a) E.g. It suggests water is as necessary for life as the Sun. *[1 mark]*
   b) Any sensible explanation, e.g. Dharker describes water using imagery of light to emphasise its beauty and life-giving quality *[1 mark]*. By comparing water to the Sun, which is essential for life on Earth, she highlights the importance of water *[1 mark]*.

6 You should have explained how the poem's form reflects the event described in the poem.
1-2 marks for a simple answer that explains how the poem's form reflects the event in the poem.
3-4 marks for a well-developed answer that clearly explains how the poem's form reflects the event in the poem.
Here is an example of a point you may have made: Dharker reflects the increase in water after the pipe bursts, from a "drip" to a "rush", by increasing the length of the poem's stanzas. The poem begins with two short stanzas where Dharker describes the lack of water, but then expands into a much longer middle stanza when the pipe bursts. Dharker also uses enjambment in the third and fourth stanzas to reflect the flow of water described in the poem. The use of enjambment also mirrors the chaos of the people running about in the village as they try to catch some of the precious water.

7 You should have used details from the text to explain how the poem's tone changes.
1-2 marks for a simple answer that uses some detail from the text to explain how the poem's tone changes.
3-4 marks for a well-developed answer that uses detail from the text to clearly explain how the poem's tone changes.
Here is an example of a point you may have made: The poem begins with a wistful, pitiful tone, as the narrator instructs the reader to "Imagine" the beautiful sound of a drip of water in a place where there "never is enough water". However, when the pipe bursts the tone becomes excited and joyful as the narrator describes the people rushing to the burst pipe and children "screaming" with pleasure as the water "sings" over their bodies.

8 You should have used details from the text to explain how Dharker presents water as a religious force.

1-3 marks for a simple answer that uses some details from the text to explain how Dharker presents water as a religious force.
4-6 marks for a well-developed answer that is supported by details from the text to explain how Dharker presents water as a religious force.
7-8 marks for a very developed answer that is well-supported by details from the text to clearly explain how Dharker presents water as a religious force.

Here are some points and explanations you might have included:
- The title of the poem is 'Blessing'. This implies that the event described in the poem, a water pipe bursting, is a gift from God.
- Dharker uses a metaphor to describe the sound of water dripping as "the voice of a kindly god". This metaphor makes water seem to be not just a blessing from God, but a part of God itself.
- Dharker uses a metaphor to describe the bursting of the water pipe as a "sudden rush / of fortune". This imagery makes the event seem like it is a miracle.
- The rushing people are described as a "congregation", which is a group of people gathered for religious worship. This suggests that the people are worshipping water as if it is their god.
- The poem ends with the lines: "the blessing sings / over their small bones." This imagery suggests that the children are being blessed by the flow of water. This could also conjure an image of some religious initiation ceremonies, where people are sprinkled or immersed in water to symbolise their admission into a faith.

Page 49 — Reading Review

1   a)   Any sensible answer, e.g. He disagrees with the plan and wants to stop it *[1 mark]*.
    b)   Any sensible answer, e.g. Macbeth doesn't want to kill the king because he has been honoured by him recently *[1 mark]*. Macbeth also believes he shouldn't risk losing his good reputation *[1 mark]*.
2   a)   Any sensible explanation, e.g. Lady Macbeth uses personification to suggest that Macbeth's ambition and hope have diminished *[1 mark]*. She compares his former willingness to act to a "drunk" man who is only brave due to alcohol, and once he's sober is "green and pale", and too scared to act *[1 mark]*. She thinks that this will persuade Macbeth to go through with the plan, because he doesn't want to be seen as a coward *[1 mark]*.
    b)   You should have used details from the text to explain other ways in which Lady Macbeth attempts to persuade Macbeth.
         1-2 marks for a simple answer that uses some detail from the text to explain how Lady Macbeth tries to persuade Macbeth.
         3-4 marks for a well-developed answer that uses detail from the text to clearly explain how Lady Macbeth tries to persuade Macbeth.
         Here is an example of a point you may have made: Lady Macbeth uses several rhetorical questions to persuade Macbeth. For example, she asks him "Art thou afeard", as this will make him want to answer 'no' and therefore go through with the plan to prove he isn't scared.
3   You should have used details from the text to describe the tone of Lady Macbeth's dialogue.
    1-2 marks for a simple answer that uses some detail from the text to describe the tone of Lady Macbeth's dialogue.
    3-4 marks for a well-developed answer that uses detail from the text to clearly describe the tone of Lady Macbeth's dialogue.
    Here is an example of a point you may have made: Lady Macbeth's dialogue is mocking in tone. For example, she repeatedly mocks Macbeth for being a "coward" and feeling "afeard" of going through with the plot. Towards the end of the extract, her tone becomes more encouraging. She answers Macbeth's question "If we should fail?" with the reassuring phrase "we'll not fail".
4   Any sensible answer, e.g. Macbeth feels frustrated in these lines *[1 mark]* because he has made his mind up and wants Lady Macbeth to stop trying to persuade him *[1 mark]*.
5   Any sensible answer, e.g. Lady Macbeth's description of what she would do to the baby is extremely shocking. *[1 mark]* The idea that a mother would have "plucked" her baby from her breast and "dashed" its brains out to keep a promise is deeply disturbing *[1 mark]*. This shocking image is highlighted by the contrast between the description of the "tender" sense of "love" felt when breast-feeding a baby, and the violent verb "dashed" that follows *[1 mark]*.
6   You should have identified and explained two ways the characters should speak and move in the final four lines of the extract to emphasise their feelings. Here are some points you may have made: I think that Macbeth should sigh and shake his head when he says "If we should fail?" *[1 mark]*. This would reflect his worry and uncertainty towards Lady Macbeth's plot *[1 mark]*. I think that Lady Macbeth should put her hands on Macbeth's shoulders and stare into Macbeth's eyes as she says her final two lines in a firm manner *[1 mark]*. This would emphasise Lady Macbeth's determination to persuade Macbeth, as she refuses to listen to his worries *[1 mark]*.
7   You should have used details from the text to explain the impression it gives of Macbeth.
    1-3 marks for a simple answer that uses some details from the text to explain your impression of Macbeth.
    4-6 marks for a well-developed answer that is supported by details from the text to explain your impression of Macbeth.
    7-8 marks for a very developed answer that is well-supported by details from the text to clearly explain your impression of Macbeth.
    Here are some points and explanations you might have included:
    - Macbeth cares about the opinions of others. At the beginning of the extract, Macbeth refuses to kill the King not because it is wrong, but simply because he is conscious not to taint his good reputation. He is also very conscious about being seen as "a man", and doesn't want to appear weak.

- He is ambitious. Macbeth cares very much about the honour he received from the King, and wants to continue to rise in status.
- He is easily provoked. Lady Macbeth succeeds at manipulating him, making him so uncomfortable he has to ask her to stop. He retaliates to her deliberately devious words.
- He is easily led. Although during Shakespeare's time a woman would normally have been subservient to a man, Lady Macbeth dominates Macbeth and seems to have persuaded him by the end of the extract.
- He is hesitant. Macbeth has countless concerns about killing the King and rarely feels sure in his decisions, asking questions like "If we should fail?", showing he is anxious about failure.

Page 51 — Reading Review

1 Any sensible answer, e.g. The band members are women. *[1 mark]*

2 Any two sensible reasons, e.g. Much of the band's music is about how the world is an illusion *[1 mark]*. The band also present themselves as a serious rock group, but they don't actually take themselves or their music seriously *[1 mark]*.

3 a) Any one of e.g. "fractured perfection", "playfully profound", "angrily euphoric", "imperfectly polished" *[1 mark]*

   b) Any sensible answer, e.g. The use of oxymorons emphasises that the band's music is full of contradictions, *[1 mark]* reinforcing the idea that the band's music is hard to define *[1 mark]*.

   c) Any sensible answer, e.g. The writer uses a simile to compare the album to riding a "faulty roller coaster which jerks up and down" *[1 mark]*. This suggests that the album takes the listener in many different directions that are hard to predict *[1 mark]*

4 Any sensible answer, e.g. To link the conclusion to the introduction *[1 mark]* by answering the implied question in the introduction about whether or not the band will find major success *[1 mark]*.

5 You should have given three layout features from the article with explanations of why each feature has been used. Here are some features you may have included: text presented in columns, a heading, a separate introduction.

6 You should have used details from the text to explain how the band feel about school.
   1-2 marks for a simple answer that uses some detail from the text to explain how the band feel about school.
   3-4 marks for a well-developed answer that uses detail from the text to clearly explain how the band feel about school.
   Here is an example of a point you may have made: The band found their school days quite difficult at times. Ellis says that she felt the weight of her potential, suggesting that she found the high expectations of her parents and teachers to be a burden.

7 You should have used details from the text to explain whether you think the writer would give the album a perfect score.
   1-2 marks for a simple answer that uses some detail from the text to explain whether the writer would give the album a perfect score.
   3-4 marks for a well-developed answer that uses detail from the text to clearly explain whether the writer would give the album a perfect score.
   Here is an example of a point you may have made: I don't think the writer would give the album a perfect score, because while the writer is intrigued and impressed by *Dreams of Somewhere*, they also criticise the album for being too chaotic. The album leaves them "endlessly surprised and scintillated" but the result is that the listener ends up "a little shaken", suggesting that the writer isn't entirely approving of the album.

8 You should have used details from the text to explain how the writer uses language and structure to entertain the reader.
   1-3 marks for a simple answer that uses some details from the text to explain how the writer uses language and structure to entertain the reader.
   4-6 marks for a well-developed answer that is supported by details from the text to clearly explain how the writer uses language and structure to entertain the reader.
   Here are some points and explanations you might have included:
   - The author compares the band and their music to energetic natural forces such as a "roaring tornado" and a "whirlwind". This creates a sense of excitement and energy for the reader.
   - The author uses alliteration when describing the band's school days, which were full of "missed deadlines, daydreaming and detentions". This emphasises the trouble they got into at school.
   - The author weaves quotations from an interview with the band into their article to illustrate their points. This structure creates variety in the article that helps to keep the reader entertained.

Section 7: Writing — Non-Fiction Writing

Page 52 — Before you Start

1 Any sensible answers, e.g.
   Example: "As it disappeared over the horizon, colours became muted"
   Explanation: Describing the colours as "muted" helps the reader to imagine the fading of light as the sun sets.

2 Any sensible answers, e.g.
   a) Walk backwards slowly rather than running to avoid startling the bear or making it feel threatened.
   b) While exploring an area of deep water, the team spotted some sign of the squid's presence.

3 Any two of the following: exaggerating good points, rhetorical questions, list of three, alliteration and use of "we".

Page 53 — Planning

1. **a)** Any sensible rewriting of the plan that adds more detail to the point in paragraph 1, separates paragraphs 2 and 3 into more paragraphs so that there is one paragraph per point, and makes the conclusion more convincing.
   b) Any sensible answer that explains how the changes improve the plan.
2. Any sensible plan for one of the topics, e.g.
   Introduction: There are lots of reasons why crazy golf is an ideal sport to have at the Olympic Games.
   Point 1: It's much more exciting than regular golf.
   Point 2: Players need to be highly skilled.
   Point 3: Everybody has an equal opportunity to be great at it.
   Conclusion: Crazy golf should become an Olympic sport.
3. Any sensible plan that argues either for or against the idea and includes an introduction, at least three key arguments and a conclusion.

Page 54-55 — Structure

1. **a)** Any sensible answer, e.g. Here at Windshire School, there's a club for everyone. From cake appreciation to balloon modelling and line dancing — you name it, we've got it! One club that deserves a special mention is The Friends of Dogs Society.
   b) Any sensible answer, e.g. To provide an example to illustrate the point made in paragraph 2.
   c) Any sensible answer, e.g. It doesn't give any details about what The Friends of Dogs Society does even though the introduction suggests that it will.
   d) Any sensible answer, e.g. The Friends of Dogs Society was set up several years ago by a group of friends who all owned shelter dogs. They wanted to raise awareness about the importance of rehoming animals and encourage people to adopt from shelters rather than buy from a breeder.
2. Any sensible answer where the paragraphs are in a more logical order, e.g.
   Over the years, our capital city has become an increasingly popular tourist destination. In 2019, around 21.7 million people visited London, up 18% from 2015. It is therefore clear that experiencing London is a priority for travellers. One reason for this popularity is that London offers something for everyone: there are countless shops, fascinating museums and an almost endless list of restaurants.
3. **a)** Any sensible answer, e.g. Lia's bravery is shown through the way she overcomes her fear.
   b) E.g. "With a deep breath and shaking hands, she turned on her torch and swam forward."
   c) Any sensible answer, e.g. Lia's "shaking hands" suggest that she is afraid, but she swims forward into the darkness anyway, with only her torch for light.
4. **a)** Any sensible points which are clearly linked to the essay question.
   b) Any sensible conclusion that includes an answer to the question in the essay title, e.g. In conclusion, the benefits of befriending a zombie clearly outweigh those of befriending a werewolf, so I would agree with the statement. Zombies will go to any lengths to protect someone they consider an ally, so if you are able to befriend a zombie, they will reward you with their loyalty. In comparison, werewolves are solitary creatures who do not form close bonds with others, so it's more difficult to develop a close friendship with these creatures.
5. **a)** Any sensible plan that includes well-structured, logically ordered points, aimed at persuading people to get involved in the welly-throwing competition.
   b) Any sensible answer.

Page 56 — Quoting

1. **a)** A) "Balloons exploded", "a blizzard of confetti"
   B) "serenity", "unconsciousness"
   b) Any sensible answers, e.g.
   A) The description of the party presents it as a negative experience. The narrator says that "Balloons exploded" and there was "a blizzard of confetti". These violent words suggest the celebration was overwhelming.
   B) The poet finds peace when they go to sleep. They write that there's a "serenity" in "unconsciousness". This suggests that sleep is a soothing experience for them.
2. **a) i)** The quotation is in a separate sentence, so it doesn't flow.
   ii) The quotation is missing quotation marks.
   iii) The quotation doesn't match what's written in the text.
   b) Any sensible answers, e.g.
   The storm is presented as a powerful force that "roared like a mighty beast". This simile creates the impression that the storm is strong and aggressive.
   Alliteration emphasises the wind's destructive nature. The writer describes how the wind "howled, hammered and harassed" houses. The repeated 'h' sound suggests that it is relentless.
   The writer uses personification to make the wind seem more threatening. They write that the wind wanted to "infiltrate" people's homes. This word implies that the wind has no respect for others.

Pages 57-58 — Writing Essays

1. **a)** Any sensible introduction which mentions the points outlined in the plan, e.g. Time travel has fascinated and alarmed people for generations. For some, it promises a first-hand experience of life in a different time and the chance to witness some of history's most important events. For others, it would open the door to unknown threats and cause friction with those around them. Would time travel be more trouble than it's worth? Or would we be missing out on a golden opportunity?

b) Any sensible conclusion that sums up the points in the plan, e.g. In conclusion, although time travel offers a multitude of benefits such as a greater understanding of the past and real-life experience of historical events, there are still many disadvantages. It could cause rifts between loved ones, and the possibility of encountering unusual threats and diseases could have serious repercussions on the present day.

2 Any three sensible points for each essay topic, e.g.
   a) Young footballers who receive so much money so quickly become out of touch.
Top level footballers often don't know what to do with so much money.
There are other professions that are more essential in society but are underpaid.
   b) The leading actors give stunning performances which bring the story to life.
The plot is littered with twists and turns which leave you wanting more.
The special effects make you feel like everything you're watching is real.
   c) Towns should not profit from basic human needs.
It is unfair to ask parents to pay to use a changing facility for their baby.
Free access to a toilet should be a human right.
   d) The majority of people spend several hours a day on social media and other online platforms.
A lot of people consider being connected virtually as one of the most important things in life.
There are some people who actively reject the virtual world in favour of a more grounded existence.

3 a) The author uses several techniques to create an unnerving atmosphere in this extract. // The use of onomatopoeia in the first paragraph helps the reader to imagine the sounds experienced by the narrator. This allows them to build a clearer picture of what the setting is like. // The imagery used to describe the old man evokes the senses to help the reader visualise him — we can imagine the stark contrast of his colourless skin and his black clothing 'without a single speck of colour'. // His behaviour also adds to the atmosphere. He is initially portrayed as unwelcoming, but then becomes more enthusiastic after the narrator has entered his home, and this creates an unnerving atmosphere.
   b) Any sensible answer, e.g. I would add evidence such as quotes from the text to properly support the points made, and I would expand the explanations to make the structure more effective.
   c) Any sensible conclusion, e.g. In conclusion, the author uses a combination of language techniques to create an unnerving atmosphere in the extract. By appealing to the senses through onomatopoeia and imagery, he helps the reader to feel like they're experiencing what is happening.

4 a) Any sensible answer, e.g. Discuss the advantages and disadvantages of hot and cold weather.
   b) Any sensible essay which uses the points in the plan as well as your own ideas. It must include an introduction, a main body and a conclusion.

5 a) Any sensible answer, e.g. Museums have been educating society for generations, but have they lost their spark?

b) Any sensible answers, e.g. In some museums, the exhibits are often quite dated.
In some museums, not a lot of new exhibits are being added.
Existing exhibits are still interesting for people now.
Some museums are introducing new ways for people to engage with history.
You should have chosen the three strongest points to use in your essay.
   c) Any sensible answer, e.g. Whilst museums often rely on existing, older exhibits to drawn in visitors, they're still managing to innovate and attract a new generation of history lovers.
   d) Any sensible essay that uses the answers to a)-c) to discuss the prompt. It should have an introduction, three main paragraphs and a conclusion.

Page 59 — Formal and Informal Language
1 a) i) formal
     ii) informal
     iii) informal
     iv) formal
   b) Any sensible answers, e.g.
She was floored by Arthur's lousy manners.
I sprinted away from the suspicious-looking horse.
Santiago was overjoyed about receiving some exquisite food.
Jo called on Malachi for a natter.

2 a) You should have underlined:
<u>Thanks for gathering here today</u>. I'm going to discuss the important matter of installing vending machines in our school. These machines are vital to the happiness of students and teachers alike, as they provide us with various delicacies and <u>pick-me-ups</u> throughout the day. Some <u>folks</u> would argue that the treats commonly found in vending machines are <u>junk</u>, but I propose that healthy alternatives be provided alongside the <u>usual suspects</u> like chocolate bars and sweets. This would encourage thought about having a more balanced lifestyle.
   b) Any sensible answer, e.g. Thank you for gathering here today. I am going to discuss the important matter of installing vending machines in our school. These machines are vital to the happiness of students and teachers alike, as they provide us with various delicacies and refreshments to sustain our energy throughout the day. Though some would argue that the treats commonly found in vending machines are detrimental to our health, I propose that healthy alternatives be provided alongside the more typical options of chocolate bars and sweets. This would encourage thought about having a more balanced lifestyle.

3 Any sensible answer, e.g.
Dear Mr Anderson,
I would be delighted if you were to hire me as a receptionist at your law firm. I am a very organised person and I always work hard. I have extensive work experience, including several months at a restaurant, and I currently volunteer at my local library. They may not be positions in the legal sector, but I believe they provide me with useful skills that will give me an advantage over other candidates.
Yours sincerely,
Julius Weber

Pages 60-61 — Writing to Inform, Explain and Advise

1. **a)** You should have circled: to inform
   b) It provides details of where and when the hiking trip will take place.
   It tells people what they need to bring with them on the trip.
2. Any sensible answer that includes all the points in the list and explains why they made the holiday fun.
3. **a)** Any sensible answer, e.g. You could talk about the skills you have gained from your hobby or club, like commitment, or social skills .
   b) Any sensible text which advises students about what skills they might need to join the club.
4. Any sensible answer that includes all of the facts and figures given in the boxes.
5. **a)** to advise
   b) Any sensible answer, e.g. The text contains plenty of well-supported recommendations that advise the reader about how to attract more pollinators to their garden.
   c) Any sensible answer that includes a clear purpose for one of the topics given and provides the main features of its text type.

Pages 62-63 — Writing to Persuade and Argue

1. Any sensible answers, e.g.
   a) Book your stay now — you'll love our amazing family-friendly facilities.
   b) Do you enjoy outdoor sports? Then you'll love visiting the woodland activity centre.
   c) Why settle for a boring, run-of-the-mill cheddar when you can have a mouth-watering brie?
2. Any sensible answer that includes all of the arguments provided.
3. **a)** Any sensible answers, e.g.
   People who say ham and pineapple is more interesting than other pizza toppings have clearly never experimented with all the delicious toppings at their disposal.
   Some people enjoy the contrast of sweet and savoury food, but a pizza is a savoury food and ought to remain that way.
   The texture of warm pineapple is not a pleasant one and it spoils the overall experience of eating a pizza.
   b) Any sensible text which uses the arguments in part a).
4. **a)** Any sensible answer, e.g. Text A is more convincing because it gives multiple reasons to back up its argument while using definite language like "would" and "will". Text B uses words like "could", which suggests there's doubt about whether what it's saying is true.
   b) Any sensible answer, e.g. It's clear that video games offer a more immersive experience than board games. The crisp graphics of virtual reality allow players to become part of an artificial world and feel a more physical connection to what they're playing. It's impossible to replicate this with a standard board game, which relies solely on imagination. Video game plots are also much more exciting and involve a wider range of characters, giving players more freedom to express themselves virtually.
5. Any sensible answer which uses the points in the box to either argue in favour of or against banning mobile phones in schools.

Section 8: Writing — Fiction Writing

Page 64 — Before you Start

1. **a)** The silence in the hall attested to the fact that the crowd had been enchanted by the speaker's wisdom. — **D**
   A veil of red velvet curtains drew back to reveal ornate cardboard scenery and old-fashioned furniture. — **B**
   The corridors, full of exhausted employees, were a labyrinth of harsh lighting and tired carpets. — **A**
   Beady eyes turned expectantly to the stage as the chime of champagne flutes hushed. — **C**
   b) Any sensible answer that uses the setting and graphic to describe a character.
2. Any sensible answers that build on the story idea.

Page 65 — Planning

1. **a)** E.g. It doesn't provide detail so the writer will need to stop and come up with what to include when they are actually writing.
   b) Any sensible answers, e.g. The plan could be more precise, rather than giving different options. It could also be more thorough — large parts of the plot are missing.
   c) Any sensible plan that includes the suggested changes.
2. **a)** Any sensible answer, e.g. It summarises exactly what is going to happen in the story. The ending has been planned so the writer knows what they're aiming for.
   b) Any sensible answers.

Page 66 — Structure

1. When a story jumps back in time, this is called a **flashback**. When it jumps ahead in time, this is called a **flashforward**. Sometimes, authors will use a **cliffhanger** to help keep readers totally gripped by the story. A split **narrative** is a story told from two different **perspectives**.
2. **a)** Grandma's famous pizza recipe is stolen from the locked safe.
   Written on the wall in tomato sauce is "It's my turn to get a slice of the pie. Your pizzeria will never make any dough again, as long as I live."
   Across the road, she sees a hooded figure with a tomato-stained piece of paper.
   Armed with her rolling pin, Grandma follows them, shouting for them to stop.
   The figure responds to Grandma's shouts by throwing pepperoni at her.
   b) Any sensible answers which build on the previous plot points.
   c) C — it uses a mysterious rhetorical question which engages the reader and makes them want to read on.
   d) Any sensible answer that uses an effective structure e.g. I would include a flashforward at the beginning of the story without much context to pique the reader's curiosity about how the story gets to that point.

e) Any sensible answer that includes explanation of why the chosen ending would be effective.

Page 67 — Building Character
1 a) Any sensible adjectives e.g.
    i) extroverted
    ii) perceptive
    iii) self-assured
  b) Any sensible answers that explain how your chosen adjectives reflect information about the characters given in the sentences.
2 Any sensible descriptions that build upon information and inferences from each statement.
3 Any sensible descriptions that effectively express the character traits mentioned in the texts.

Page 68 — Building Setting
1 a) Any sensible answer, e.g. It builds an intimidating and ominous atmosphere. The imagery used creates a sense of danger and unease.
  b) Any sensible answer, e.g. It could be used in an adventure story. The sinister atmosphere would work effectively in a story about a character facing a challenge and perhaps overcoming evil.
  c) Any sensible answers that effectively reflect the different genres.
2 a) i) Any sensible answer, e.g. A bedroom which is extremely untidy, with mounds of dirty laundry and used plates stacked all around.
    ii) Any sensible answer, e.g. It would create a stale and slightly grotty atmosphere, which would provide the reader with more information about the character's personality and behaviour.
  b) Any sensible answer.
3 Any sensible answers which reflect each title.

Page 69 — Writing Stories
1 a) Any sensible answers.
  b) Any sensible answers that refer to the effect of the opening sentences.
2 a) Any sensible answer.
  b) i) Any sensible answer.
    ii) Any sensible examples.
  c) Any sensible answer.
3 a) Any sensible plan that considers character, structure, point of view and atmosphere.
  b) Any sensible answer.

Page 70 — Writing Scripts
1 Any sensible answers.
2 a) Any sensible answer that uses stage directions effectively.
  b) Any sensible answer.
  c) Any sensible answer that uses stage directions and dialogue effectively.
3 a) Any sensible answer that uses stage directions and dialogue effectively.
  b) Any sensible answer that uses stage directions and dialogue effectively.

Page 71 — Poetry
1 a) 10 syllables
  b) i) Any sensible answer, e.g. serene, mysterious, peaceful
    ii) In a poem about daytime, I would make the mood less peaceful and more busy.

  c) Any sensible answer.
  d) Any sensible answer.
2 a) Any sensible answer which fits the poem's rhyme scheme and contains 8 syllables.
  b) Any sensible answer which continues the rhyme scheme and contains 8 syllables in each line.
3 Any sensible answer which meets every point on the checklist.

Section 9: Writing — Writing Properly

Page 72 — Before you Start
1 You should have ticked: a), c), d) and e)
2 You should have circled: comparitive, neccessery and accomodate.
  The correct spellings are: comparative, necessary and accommodate.
3 a) The sentence should use a dash or a colon instead of a semi-colon.
    E.g. I will need several items to reach that ball: a rope, a ladder and a big stick.
  b) The sentence punctuates direct speech incorrectly. 'He' shouldn't be capitalised but 'they' should be.
    "Somebody devoured all the cupcakes!" he roared. "They were on the counter!"
  c) There should be a hyphen between "well" and "known".
    It is a well-known fact that camping holidays are superior to all others.

Page 73 — Structuring Your Writing
1 Any sensible answer, e.g. Text A uses short sentences — this creates a faster pace that reflects Timo's adrenaline. Text B uses one long sentence punctuated by a comma. This creates a slower pace that mirrors the careful task of sewing.
2 Anjeli turned the corner of the maze to find another dead end.
    [1] "We'll never get out," she groaned. But her brother Farhan was undeterred.
    [2] "Don't say that," he said, turning back around. "We'll jut try again."
    3] Anjeli resignedly trudged after him. Only an hour ago, she had been standing atop a hill looking down at the maze, thinking that navigating it would be easy. [4] But amidst the towering hedges, her confidence dwindled.
    [5] Finally, they reached another corner. Anjeli's eyes were unexpectedly blinded by sunlight pouring through a wide gap.
  [1] — New paragraph for new person speaking.
  [2] — New paragraph for new person speaking.
  [3] — New paragraph for changing character focus.
  [4] — Remove unnecessary new paragraph.
  [5] — New paragraph for jump forward in time.
3 a) Any sensible introduction, e.g. This speech will argue the advantages of using robots to carry out day-to-day tasks.
  b) Any two sensible changes, e.g. The second paragraph should use examples to make the arguments clearer and well-supported. There should be linking words at the start of both paragraphs to make them flow.

c) i) Any sensible answer, e.g. The new information introduced in the final sentence should be moved out of the conclusion and put into the body of the speech. The conclusion should also sum up the main arguments made in the speech. As the speech covers both the benefits and drawbacks of robots, the conclusion should weigh up these arguments, rather than just focusing on the benefits of robots.

ii) Any sensible conclusion, e.g. In conclusion, while it is clear that robots can be very useful in helping people carry out basic chores, the development of robots could be hampered by concerns that they may become too intelligent.

Page 74 — Redrafting and Proofreading

1 a) Any sensible answer, e.g. The phone was ringing loudly downstairs. Alice ignored it at first, but it kept on ringing. It seemed to be getting louder, so she finally got up from her bed and answered it.

b) Any sensible sentence, e.g. Without hesitation, Alice reached for the bag and marched off, headed for the woods.

c) Any sensible redrafted version of the extract, e.g.
The phone was ringing loudly downstairs. Alice ignored it at first, but it kept on ringing. It seemed to be getting louder, so she finally got up from her bed and answered it.
"Hello?" she said. Silence. "Hello?" she repeated, wariness creeping into her voice. Still no response. Alice was about to hang up when the other end of the line crackled into life.
"Alice," a familiar voice whispered, "don't ask any questions. Just go to my room, grab my bag and meet me in the woods." Without hesitation, Alice reached for the bag and marched off, headed for the woods.

2 a) Radio stations are being encoureged to stop playing 'Dance-aster'; a song that entered the charts last tuesday. The tune, predicted to be a global sensasion, is now a global frustration, some who hear it find themselves unable to stop dancing. Earlier this afternoon: a local supermarket had to close after a group of shopper's effected by the tune trampled the entire fruit and vegatable section to a pulp.
"It was unbelieveably bizarre." remarked one witness, who wishes to remain anonimous.
If youre wondering how to deal with people overpowered by the need to groove, they're are some things you can do; keep your distance, try to turn the song of, or dance along with them!

b) Radio stations are being **encouraged** to stop playing 'Dance-aster', a song that entered the charts last **Tuesday**. The tune, predicted to be a global **sensation**, is now a global frustration**. Some** who hear it find themselves unable to stop dancing. Earlier this afternoon**,** a local supermarket had to close after a group of shoppers **affected** by the tune trampled the entire fruit and **vegetable** section to a pulp.
"It was **unbelievably** bizarre," remarked one witness, who wishes to remain **anonymous**.
If **you're** wondering how to deal with people overpowered by the need to groove, **there** are some things you can do**:** keep your distance, try to turn the song **off**, or dance along with them!

Section 10: Writing — Making It Interesting

Page 75 — Before you Start

1 Any sensible words which have a similar meaning, e.g.
a) extremely
b) commence
c) authorise
d) furious
e) colossal
f) mutter

2 Any sensible synonyms of the words in brackets, e.g. The shire horse **plodded** steadily down the dusty farm track, **lugging** a cart laden with fresh produce destined for the local market. A **refreshing** breeze **wafted** through the fields of wheat. High in the sky, the sun **shimmered** brightly, casting golden shadows across the landscape. The **weary** farmer yawned and drove the horse on.

3 a) i) Start each sentence in a different way.
ii) Split the sentence into two separate sentences.
iii) Avoid repetition of the word 'ugly'.

b) Any sensible answers which use the improvements suggested in part a), e.g.
It was half past midnight when I woke up. A gale was blowing outside, which caused the windows to rattle violently. My bedroom was ice-cold.
Nobody had expected it to be such a spectacular show. The actors weren't very well known and the director had never worked on such a huge production before.
The wallpaper they'd chosen was unbelievably ugly. It had hideous swirling patterns in unsightly colours which made the living room look horrible.

Page 76 — Using Different Techniques

1 Any sensible answers, e.g.
a) Anyone who attempted the stunt needed to be ice-cool in the face of jeopardy.
b) The children didn't notice the hours slipping away while they were playing.
c) I was paralysed with fear after touring the haunted house.
d) "No problem," said the mechanic. "I'll have this fixed before you can say 'overalls'."

2 Any sensible comparisons which complete the sentences, e.g.
a) The diamond shone like slivers of light on a rippling stream.
b) Mike's scooter is faster than a rocket blasting off.
c) My parrot sings more melodically than a world-class opera singer.
d) The gloves are as soft as a rabbit's fluffy white tail.
e) Her hair was like a golden waterfall cascading down her back.

3   Any sensible answer, e.g. Sarah was sitting in a chair on the patio, listening fondly to the birdsong that was echoing from the nearby trees. She watched a blackbird hop agilely across the lawn. It paused, looking for the tell-tale wriggle of worms among the blades of grass. It dropped its head in a blur, and came up with a writhing worm which was protesting its fate.

Page 77 — Figurative Language

1   Any sensible answers, e.g.
- a) We waited for an eternity to get into the aquarium.
- b) The suitcase weighed a ton.

2   Any sensible answers that use the figurative language technique mentioned in the question. Each sentence should appeal to a different sense. E.g.
- a) The disco ball was a glittering star on the ceiling.
- b) The wind chime tinkled in the evening breeze.
- c) This ice cream is a fabulously fruity treat.

3   Any sensible answers, e.g.
- a) The crowded train carriage was an oven, stuffed with hot bodies. The open doors released a short gust of hot air before closing again, sealing everyone inside.
- b) The trees were soldiers standing in a line, stretching as far as the eye could see in both directions. The leafy battalion screened the hills from the lowland fields.

4   Any sensible answer that uses any 3 figurative language techniques.

Section 11: Writing Review

Page 78 — Writing Review

1
- a) Any sensible answer, e.g. A tense atmosphere in which the characters feel anxious about being caught *[1 mark]*.
- b) Any sensible stage direction, e.g. "(*The criminals creep along a dark alleyway. A siren wails in the distance.*)" *[1 mark]*

2
- a) Any sensible adjectives, three for each criminal *[2 marks]*
- b) Any sensible answer, e.g. dopey — The character could knock something over or misunderstand another character's instructions *[1 mark per character]*.
- c) Any sensible answer that summarises their relationship *[2 marks]*.
- d) Any sensible stage direction that reflects this relationship *[1 mark]*.

3
- a) Any sensible answer, e.g. the characters want to buy a luxurious holiday home *[1 mark]*.
- b) Any sensible explanation, e.g. The characters are robbing the bank out of greed rather than need, so they might take more money than they need to buy the holiday home *[1 mark]*.

4   Any sensible plan, e.g.
Engaging opening — Josie and Aleks are outside a bank in the middle of the night *[1 mark]*.
Plot development 1 — The criminals break in and look for the vault *[1 mark]*.
Plot development 2 — One character accidentally sets off the alarm and alerts the neighbours to their presence *[1 mark]*.
Plot development 3 — The criminals quickly pack their bag with cash, not realising there is a hole in it *[1 mark]*.
Satisfying ending — The criminals get away but unknowingly drop all the money out of the bag as they escape, so they end up with nothing *[1 mark]*.

5   Any script that does the following:
- Uses the plan from question 4 effectively.
- Follows a logical structure — it must have an engaging opening, several sensible plot developments and a satisfying ending.
- Describes an appropriate setting to create a particular atmosphere.
- Includes two characters that are suitable for the story, and explores the relationship between them.
- Uses stage directions and dialogue to tell the story.
- Uses stage directions and dialogue to reflect the characters' personalities.
- Uses correct spelling, punctuation and grammar.
- Uses a variety of sentence structures and interesting vocabulary.

[10 marks]

Page 79 — Writing Review

1
- a) Any sensible answer, e.g. It should have a critical and persuasive tone as it is arguing an opinion *[2 marks]*.
- b) Any sensible answer, e.g. Use persuasive techniques like statistics, emotive language and rhetorical questions *[2 marks]*.

2
- a) Any sensible plan presenting an opinion, e.g.
Introduction: There are lots of reasons why graffiti should not be punished.
[1 mark]
Argument 1: It requires artistic talent, which should not be punished but encouraged.
[1 mark]
Argument 2: Many graffiti artworks have become a positive part of the community, like those by Banksy.
[1 mark]
Argument 3: It often reflects the views of the people that live there, and it is their right to express these views. *[1 mark]*
Conclusion: Graffiti should not be seen as a crime, but admired and respected as self-expression.
[1 mark]
- b) Any sensible plan that develops the points in question 2 with clear evidence for each point.

3
- a) Any sensible reason e.g. Some may feel that there is a lack of skill in graffiti. *[1 mark]*
- b) Any sensible response, e.g. Some street art works have become famous for being so impressive. We should celebrate artistic talent. *[2 marks]*

4   Any opinion piece that does the following:
- Follows a plan effectively.
- Follows a logical structure — it must have an engaging introduction, several sensible arguments following a logical order and a convincing conclusion.
- Links paragraphs together so that the arguments flow smoothly.
- Uses evidence (e.g. statistics) to back up each point and includes a detailed explanation.
- Uses persuasive techniques to argue its points, e.g. rhetorical questions, direct speech or repetition.
- Includes a counter-argument with reasons and evidence why it is wrong.
- Uses an appropriate tone throughout the article.
- Uses correct spelling, punctuation and grammar.
- Uses a variety of sentence structures and interesting vocabulary.

[10 marks]

Page 80-81 — Writing Review

Use the information below to help you mark your writing tasks.

Task 1 — Your speech should include: your attitude towards the use of detentions as a punishment *[1 mark]*, reasons why you hold this view, backed up with evidence *[2 marks]* and reasons why others might disagree with you, followed by counter-arguments to these reasons *[1 mark]*. Your speech should be aimed at other school children *[1 mark]* and it should persuade the reader *[1 mark]*. It should also include interesting vocabulary *[1 mark]* and a range of sentence structures *[1 mark]*. The spelling, punctuation and grammar should be accurate (if you've made some mistakes, give yourself 1 mark) *[2 marks]*.

Task 2 — Your description should include: details which reflect the photograph *[1 mark]*, figurative language *[2 marks]* and language which builds the atmosphere created in the photo *[2 marks]*. Your description should entertain the reader *[1 mark]*. It should also include interesting vocabulary *[1 mark]* and a range of sentence structures *[1 mark]*. The spelling, punctuation and grammar should be accurate (if you've made some mistakes, give yourself 1 mark) *[2 marks]*.

Task 3 — Your leaflet should include: useful information about the club *[1 mark]*, a brief description of the art club's role in the community *[1 mark]*, reasons why people should join the club *[1 mark]* and a clear structure and layout *[2 marks]*. Your leaflet should use informative techniques, e.g. facts, statistics, clear language *[1 mark]*. It should also include interesting vocabulary *[1 mark]* and a range of sentence structures *[1 mark]*. The spelling, punctuation and grammar should be accurate (if you've made some mistakes, give yourself 1 mark) *[2 marks]*.

Task 4 — Your description should include: a focus on an introverted character *[1 mark]*, details about the character's appearance *[1 mark]*, description of what the character says and does *[1 mark]* and an exploration of the character's thoughts and feelings *[2 marks]*. Your description should entertain the reader *[1 mark]*. It should also include interesting vocabulary *[1 mark]* and a range of sentence structures *[1 mark]*. The spelling, punctuation and grammar should be accurate (if you've made some mistakes, give yourself 1 mark) *[2 marks]*.

Task 5 — Your letter should include: suggestions for a variety of facilities in the youth zone *[1 mark]*, reasons why you think they would be suitable *[2 marks]* and evidence to support the reasons you have given *[1 mark]*. Your leaflet should be aimed at council members *[1 mark]* and it should advise the reader *[1 mark]*. It should also include interesting vocabulary *[1 mark]* and a range of sentence structures *[1 mark]*. The spelling, punctuation and grammar should be accurate (if you've made some mistakes, give yourself 1 mark) *[2 marks]*.

Task 6 — Your story should include: details about a celebration *[1 mark]*, figurative language *[1 mark]*, interesting structural devices *[1 mark]* and vivid characters and settings *[2 marks]*. Your description should entertain the reader *[1 mark]*. It should also include interesting vocabulary *[1 mark]* and a range of sentence structures *[1 mark]*. The spelling, punctuation and grammar should be accurate (if you've made some mistakes, give yourself 1 mark) *[2 marks]*.